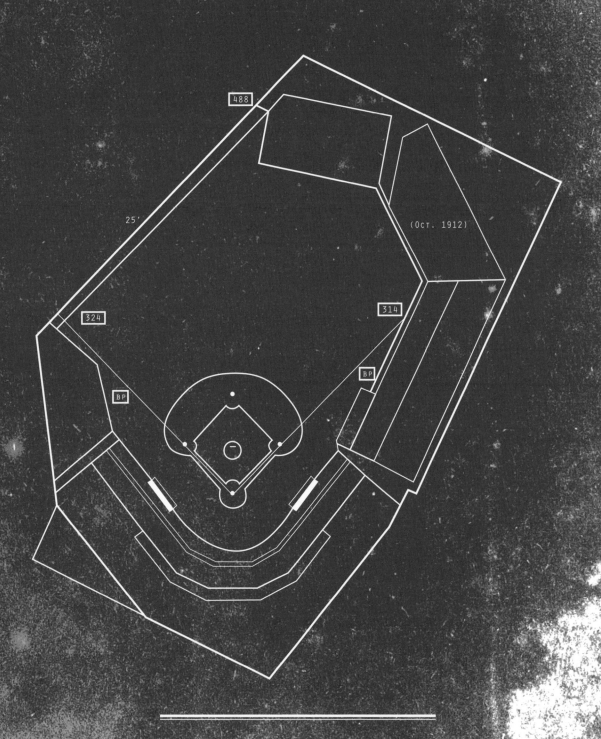

FENWAY PARK

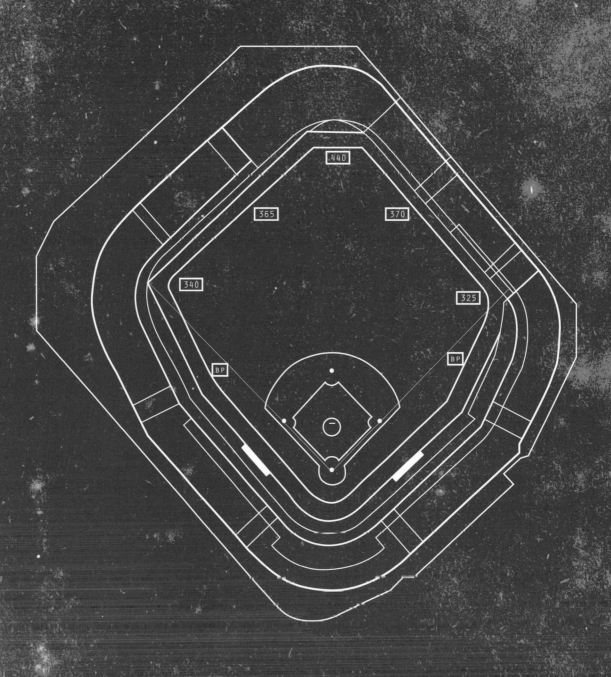

TIGER STADIUM

AMERICA'S CLASSIC

Ballparks

AMERICA'S CLASSIC

Ballparks

A Collection of Images and Memorabilia

JAMES BUCKLEY JR.

THUNDER BAY
P·R·E·S·S

San Diego, California

Thunder Bay Press
An imprint of the Baker & Taylor Publishing Group
10350 Barnes Canyon Road, San Diego, CA 92121
www.thunderbaybooks.com

All notations of errors or omissions should be addressed to Thunder Bay Press, Editorial Department, at the above address. All other correspondence (author inquiries, permissions) concerning the content of this book should be addressed to becker&mayer! Books, 11120 NE 33rd Place, Suite 101, Bellevue, WA 98004.

America's Classic Ballparks is produced by becker&mayer!, Bellevue, Washington. www.beckermayer.com

Note: All removable documents and memorabilia are reproductions of original items and are not originals themselves.

Editor: Dana Youlin
Designers: Katie Benezra and Rosebud Eustace
Photo researcher: Katie del Rosario
Production coordinator: Shirley Woo
Managing editor: Michael del Rosario

ISBN-13: 978-1-60710-725-5
ISBN-10: 1-60710-725-2

Printed in China

1 2 3 4 5 17 16 15 14 13 12

FRONTISPIECE: As they have since 1912, fans pack Fenway Park on a summer evening, filling seats used by their great-grandparents and continuing a long baseball tradition.

PAGE 176: The view from the upper left field corner of the original Yankee Stadium shows why the mighty edifice was a source of such awe to millions of fans.

CONTENTS

Yankee Stadium stood above (literally) all the ballparks we'll visit in this book. For size, grandeur, and its numerous momentous occasions, Yankee looms large in baseball history.

INTRODUCTION

What is it about a ballpark?

Not a stadium, though some ballparks carry that name.

Not an arena; they're too dark and spooky.

Not a gym, even though some of the older ones carry a sweaty waft of nostalgia.

Not even a field, as in soccer or lacrosse. They're just grass with lines.

No, we mean a ballpark. A park in which people play ball. Could anything be more pleasant? Though in person the grass might not be perfect, the dirt a little scuffed up, and the cement beneath our feet a little sticky, in our mind's eye, the grass is emerald green, the dirt is raked to Buddhist perfection, and the air is redolent with popcorn, hot dogs, and joy.

Ballparks remain the most celebrated of our athletic venues. Few people retain the sort of misty-eyed memory of a football stadium, and while basketball gyms might have a few fans, other than perhaps the old Boston Garden and that place where they filmed *Hoosiers*, they don't create the same sense of emotional connection.

Ballparks are where we went with our dads. Ballparks are where we first saw a ball soar in the air, either high above our heads with a glove rising waveringly to meet it or from the side, impossibly lofty, the proverbial "major-league pop-up."

Ballparks are where we go to connect with eight-plus generations, linking current America to past America in a way that almost nothing can match. For more than a century, newly arrived citizens could find common ground with their new neighbors at the ballpark, even if they didn't know foul from fair.

And for that same century-plus, the ballpark is where a family can come together. No TV show, movie, or amusement park can offer the same combination of thrills to see, history to share, and space to talk.

But the ballpark . . . the ballpark is in a league of its own. You enter and find your seat and time sort of slows down. The pace of the game dictates the pace of conversation. And converse you will; at a ball game everyone around you is part of your party. Got a question about a stat? Someone nearby knows. Want to swap foul-ball stories? Everyone's got one. It's like bringing your neighborhood to the bleachers.

And in front of you, in a stately pace with rituals aplenty, grown men play a game. That they play it at a level only dreamed of by the rest of us doesn't seem to matter. As was said so eloquently in *Bull Durham*, "You hit the ball, you catch the ball, you throw the ball." It's a simple game.

And in this book, we celebrate the simple places where it's played. They range from the bandbox to the coliseum, from the now-vanished to the still-proudly standing. They are—or were—buildings, with doors and walls and rooms. But they are so much more than concrete and steel and wood; ballparks are a place where we feel comfortable, where we belong, where our families have gathered since the days before cars.

What is it about a ballpark? It's ours.

After all, of course . . . the whole object of the game is to go home.

★

The fellas here not only show off the finest in early 20th-century haberdashery, but they're also witnessing one of the most famous games ever at the Polo Grounds—the one-game playoff for the 1908 N.L. pennant.

★

CHAPTER ONE

THE AGE OF STEEL

1909–1914

They built them . . . and we came.

When you next visit a ballpark, you can either thank or curse William Cammeyer. His name doesn't normally pop up when you consider early baseball pioneers. He was not a team owner, nor a pioneering player, nor a popular scribe or manager. Instead, Cammeyer owned an ice rink in Brooklyn.

Of course, for much of the year, an ice rink in Brooklyn is not a big moneymaker. As spring sent his customers heading to the nearby grassy park, Cammeyer had a revelation. He put up a fence around the rink area, installed some benches, set up a booth to sell tickets . . . and where once was ice, he put in a baseball diamond.

And thus the ballpark was born.

Baseball had been played on diamonds in parks for decades by the time Cammeyer sold his first ticket on May 16, 1862. (Like a modern-day app maker,

The fans themselves formed the contours of the diamond in this 1865 woodcut. The two teams are the Philadelphia Athletics and the self-proclaimed "world's champion" Brooklyn Atlantics.

Cammeyer opened the place up for free on May 15 and then started charging a dime the next day.) People had long stood around the edges of fields to watch games, and a few folks had asked for money from the fans. But until Cammeyer's melted ice turned into the glorious grass of what Cammeyer called the Union Grounds, and it cost money to sit down, there had never been a ballpark anywhere.

Over the ensuing decades, the idea of making money from baseball quickly took hold. Ballparks of all shapes and sizes sprouted up in all sorts of places. This being the 19th century, the ballparks were made of wood. Most seated fewer than 10,000 people (though Sportsman's Park in St. Louis expanded to reach 12,000 in 1886). The seats were benches, rising at an angle behind home plate and stretching from perhaps third to first base. The roof above the people, if there was one, was held up by a series of view-obstructing pillars. The outfield often

was formed by people sitting in an arc rather than by fixed walls. (This led, not surprisingly, to the occasional shenanigan; that is, hometown fans gobbling up balls hit by their guys or perhaps impeding the occasional wandering outfielder.) During these still-horsey days, fans drew up carts and wagons as well, creating mobile seating platforms, and, of course, helping to beat the crowds in the carriage parking lot after the games. They were watching games in the still-new National Association (1871) or National League (1876), along with dozens of local ball clubs playing in town leagues or even semipro teams made up of guys just getting off work.

Many ballparks didn't have locker rooms, only a handful had any sort of reserved seating, and when Lakefront Park in Chicago set aside the first box seats, the ancestors of today's luxury suites were born. (Lakefront, like some parks of the time, was encircled by a dirt track used for cycling races on off days.)

The fans were not looking for luxury, for the most part. Baseball until the years around World War I was regarded as a blue-collar sport, played by rough men in front of rough crowds. Ladies were a rare sight at

Now that's a box seat: Horse-drawn carriages pulled up along the edge of the outfield at the original Polo Grounds in 1895, offering a comfortable view of the action.

baseball games in the late 19th and early 20th centuries. Sportsman's Park was once called a "saloon with a baseball attachment." In the growing cities, working men knocked off mid-afternoon, having been at their labors from before dawn. Most games started at 3 p.m., right around drinking time. Gambling, too, played a big part in the game of those days, with money flying around on both sides and gamblers often trying to influence the outcomes. Ball games were raucous, loud, and pretty wild. When opposing players ventured too near the grandstands in chase of baseballs, they might be pelted with bottles or trash. If more people showed up than there were seats, guys just hunkered down on the ground, edging right up to the foul lines and even crowding behind home plate.

This was a time (c. 1880) that the National League began to ban the sale of beer at the ballparks, hoping to improve conditions for fans and even attract women to the games. In response, the American Association (aka the Beer and Whiskey League) started in 1881 with beer sales as one of its own selling points. Back in the N.L., the Giants were the first team to try holding a Ladies Day, to which distaff fans were admitted free. They were not that successful, as the atmosphere was not that conducive to the enjoyment of women of refined tastes.

TOP: John Brush's Cincinnati temple to baseball was known as the Palace of the Fans, one of the first ballparks with any sort of ornamentation.

ABOVE: By the time this photo was taken in 1920, fans were enjoying numerous creature comforts at and around the yards, including the now-ubiquitous hot dog.

OUT OF THE ASHES

There were some glorious buildings in which to watch some of those games, though. St. George's Ground on Staten Island boasted two decks of seats beneath conical towers that rose like a forest of medieval princesses around the back of the diamond. Philadelphia's Baker Bowl sported crenellated edging atop its home-plate entrance. The Palace of the Fans in Cincinnati rose like a Roman temple atop concrete columns, though they

were to prove as ephemeral as the empire by which they were inspired.

The banners flew, the fans packed the parks, the horses added their own contributions to the atmosphere, things were a little rowdy, but the wooden ballparks were just fine.

For a while.

By the end of the 1800s, the combination of a series of disastrous fires and the growing appetite of the public for baseball, along with the birth in 1901 of the second Major League, the American, led team owners to search for a new way to construct their ballparks. The parks needed to be bigger to hold more fans and offer more comfort for the gentry. (And since admission was basically the only revenue for teams—no T-shirts or TV packages yet!—the bigger the better.) The parks needed to be made of something that would not burn down every 10 years or so. They needed to be built in such a way that a forest of pillars supporting the grandstand roof did not cut off the view of every 10th or 20th person. And they needed to be built in such a way as to remove the chance of freeloading. As noted in *Green Cathedrals*, Boston's South End Grounds took advantage of a new invention in 1876 when it strung "barb fence armor"

While barbed wire kept out the riffraff, the soaring turrets of Boston's South End Grounds invited baseball fans from all across the Hub to the city's first ballpark.

atop its wooden outline to prevent anyone from avoiding the ticket booth. Additionally, too, team owners recognized that the atmosphere had to be made more genteel to appeal to the folks who could and would pay a little more than 50 cents for a game. Attracting people with money meant making it safer for them to attend games, so teams started working harder to cut down on rowdyism. Old photos of the day show a crowd of bowler-hatted men in suits, but they don't indicate how many of those men were tipsy.

And men there were in droves in the cities where the Major Leagues played. The late-1800s Industrial Revolution was slowly transforming America from a rural to an urban land. Cities in the Northeast as well as Chicago, Detroit, and St. Louis swelled with people to man the expanding factories, including immigrants streaming over from Europe to seek their fortunes. As the century turned into the 1900s, the country turned into a land of cities. Industry and cars and subways brought millions out of the fields and into the buildings and factories. With regular jobs came leisure time, a rare concept in farm life. And with leisure time came baseball, a ready-made two-hour spectacle that even then linked the generations and provided fun, heroes, and villains for all. In city after city, the ballparks, with special note to the six featured in this book, became

Fans arriving at Philadelphia's Shibe Park got a great view of the signature tower behind home plate. **INSET:** Fans perched on the roofs of nearby buildings got a slightly different view of the distant action.

Forbes Field, the first concrete-and-steel ballpark in the N.L., was home to the Pirates from 1909 until 1970, when the team moved to Three Rivers Stadium, to the dismay of locals.

centers of life and repositories of memory where those workers went to watch grown men play.

As the first decade of the two-league Major Leagues came toward an end, a new era of ballparks arose to help owners increase attendance while also improving their product, thanks mostly to the creation by engineers of reinforced concrete. Steel rods rose up as a skeleton of a building. Wooden forms were built around them. Into the forms went concrete. The resulting reinforced building was stronger than ever, virtually fireproof, and capable, with ingenious cantilevering, of removing many of the roof-supporting poles.

HERE COME THE CLASSICS

In the next few years, ballparks, glorious ballparks, memorable ballparks, classic ballparks arose in cities all around the Northeast and Midwest. The very first steel-and-concrete palace was Shibe Park in Philadelphia. It opened for business on April 12, 1909. Concrete trim, brickwork exterior, and a crowning cupola all served to signal the beginning of a new era in ball-parks. (Remember the barbed wire? Shibe's location amid Philly's busy streets soon gave way to "wildcat

bleachers," now so well known as a fixture at Wrigley Field. Neighbors invited friends to their rooftops to enjoy a free game; they soon figured out they could invite strangers and charge a few bucks. Fans in Detroit also did some wildcatting. And it was not until 1935 that the Athletics' owners put up fences high enough to stop the practice in Philly.)

In Pittsburgh, Forbes Field popped up in 1909. Ramps, elevators, umpires' dressing rooms, and an avoidance of signage separated the Pirates' palace from other ballparks.

In Chicago, skinflint White Sox owner Charles Comiskey spared every expense he could in creating Comiskey Park in 1911, but it still cost him more than half a million dollars.

In Washington, D.C., National Park arose after fires destroyed the old home of the Senators in 1911.

Out of this era, five ballparks came to be regarded as classics, partly for their physical presence and partly for the feats and deeds that took place on their grass fields. The Polo Grounds and Ebbets Field had the advantage of playing host to two remarkably famous and successful teams. The late Tiger Stadium was a quintessential part of the city's fabric. Boston's Fenway Park and Chicago's Wrigley Field retain their characters as the quintessential "ballpark" of both myth and substance.

That quintet of ballparks from the Steel Age have earned a place in the collective consciousness of baseball as a select group of places that are shared by the sport no matter what team you root for. All built from 1911–1914, they each went on to lives filled with memories and moments, highlights and lowlights, heroes and villains. Each was most special to the people whose teams played there, but all have retained a permanent place in the game's consciousness. Of this set of five, only two—Wrigley and Fenway—remain to add to their lists of memories and to entice new generations of fans. Of the other three, well, we'll always have Manhattan, Brooklyn, and Detroit.

Fans of the Giants held the Polo Grounds in their hearts, but all of baseball looks back with fondness on the home of McGraw and Mathewson, Merkle and Snodgrass, Ott and Mays. The Polo Grounds of this era (there were earlier versions) opened in 1911, smack-dab amid what is probably not a Steel but a Golden Age of ballpark construction.

The following year that most cherished of "jewel boxes," Fenway Park, opened in Boston. Now a century old, it is as much a part of baseball as the bat, and generations of fans can't imagine the big leagues without the Fens.

On the same day that Fenway opened, the Tigers moved into a new park in Detroit, built partly in response to freeloaders making a mockery of their previous home.

At first called Navin Field, it would become Tiger Stadium and would stand until 1999.

In 1913, the place that ballpark historian Michael Gershman called a "shrine to Brooklyness" arose near Prospect Park in that sainted New York City borough. Ebbets Field, though it has gone the way of the underpaid ballplayer, is still alive in the memories of the sport.

Finally, in 1914, Wrigley Field arose in Chicago. Though the famed ivy would not flourish there for decades, the ballpark was planted firmly in the city's lore. It remains there today, like Fenway a near-living connection with the Golden Age of Steel.

The sixth ballpark featured in this collection only recently joined the Polo Grounds and Ebbets Field in the dustbin of Gotham's history. It came along almost a decade past the dawn of the Age of Steel, and it also stands apart from the other jewel boxes by its very bulk and size. Like the team that played there, Yankee Stadium stood above and beyond its contemporaries. By the time it was built in 1923, grand, mighty, and aloof, it rose above the status of mere ballpark. It was . . . a stadium.

These baseball palaces, two still standing and four extinct, represented a turning point in the sport and the nation. The game was moving toward wide respectability, no longer the domain of toughs and drunks. Couples could go to the game, kids could follow their heroes, and in the "new" ballparks—sturdy, safe, comfortable, vast—they could all watch together. As we asked in the introduction, what is it about a ballpark? As we try to answer that question, we'll explore these six classic examples and trace their origins and the history of what happened there. And we'll find out just what it is about a ballpark that has meant so much to so many people . . . and will continue to do so, even long after the last player leaves the field.

The pride of Brooklyn, the heart of the borough, Ebbets Field's distinctive brick exterior surrounded some of baseball's most memorable players . . . and fans.

Hey, get those fans off the field! Actually, they're not trespassing—at the Polo Grounds, one of the main exits was through center field so fans routinely paraded across the diamond, as they did here after a 1913 World Series game.

HE SATURDAY VENING POST

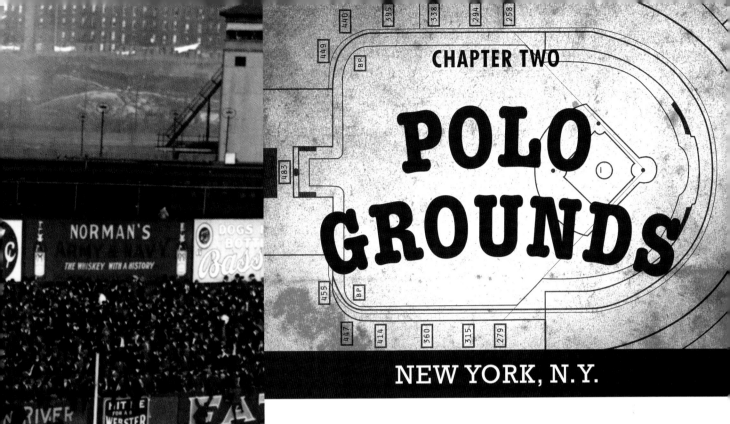

CHAPTER TWO

POLO GROUNDS

NEW YORK, N.Y.

YEAR BUILT	1911
HOME TEAMS	New York Giants, New York Yankees, New York Mets
FIRST GAME	June 28, 1911
LAST GAME	September 18, 1963 (Mets)
CAPACITY (AVERAGE)	56,000
FAMOUS FEATURES	Enormous center field, stairs to clubhouse in outfield, last big-league ballpark in Manhattan

The island of Manhattan boasts a wide set of the world's most diverse human experiences packed onto a landform just 13.4 miles long and 2.3 miles wide. You can eat food from just about any country. You can shop 24 hours a day. You can hear music, walk in parks, rent bicycles, and watch basketball games. It has special districts for everything from fur and flowers to Indian food and stockbroking. There's even a whole store that sells nothing but M&M's.

What you can't do in Manhattan, however, and what has been impossible since 1957 on the world's

Here in 1891, the Giants (on the left) welcomed the Boston Beaneaters on opening day at their new ballpark at the Polo Grounds. It was on the same site, but not the same building, as what would become the most famous Polo Grounds.

most famous island, is watch big-league baseball. As the song says, "there used to be a ballpark right there."

Near the far northern end of Manhattan, above the top reaches of Central Park, the Polo Grounds was the home of the New York Giants of the National League. From 1883 until they joined the then-Brooklyn Dodgers in colonizing California for Major League Baseball, the Giants were the main home team at the Polo Grounds and the team of choice for Manhattanites of every station. The ballpark also was home to the New York Yankees for a time, as well as being the site of boxing matches and football games of all sorts—American, association, and even Gaelic. But it was as a ballpark, built for baseball, that the Polo Grounds had its greatest fame, home to some of the most iconic events and

glorious heroes of the game's history. Indeed, few sites in baseball saw as many historic moments as the ballpark beneath Coogan's Bluff.

POLO, ANYONE?

Actually, there were several Polo Grounds that played host to Giants games. The original Polo Grounds gave its name to all the rest of them, but it was not actually built for baseball. Publisher James Gordon Bennett Jr. loaned the nascent Giants baseball team part of his polo fields at 110th Street and Fifth Avenue for the team to play its home games. The fields had previously hosted an earlier team called the Metropolitans, which joined the smaller American Association in 1883, while a new team arose to join the N.L. Originally called the

Gothams, they became the Giants not long after. The makeshift grandstands adorning Bennett's polo fields witnessed almost all of the Giants home games until 1889. Attempting to carry the island's street grid even farther north, the city of New York essentially took over Bennett's fields, extending Fifth Avenue right through the field itself.

After brief stops at temporary homes, the team found a new location at 155th Street and Eighth Avenue, even farther uptown in Manhattan. In 1890, the N.L. Giants played on the site in one ballpark, while the upstart Players' League team, also called the Giants, played on a field abutting the other. It was a strange year, as fans could sometimes watch both games at once if they had a seat high enough in the short bleachers.

Manhattan as an island is basically flat, with a few spots of gradually rising land below Central Park and some riverside bluffs and heights on its northwest side. The Harlem River coursed across the top of the island for centuries. In the 1870s, however, as more land was needed by a growing population, parts of the river were

TOP: High atop Coogan's Bluff, fans without tickets (and with extremely good eyesight) peered down on the Polo Grounds during the historic 1905 World Series.

ABOVE: Had those fans been seated above home plate on the first base side, they would have had this much better view of Christy Mathewson on the mound for the Giants.

filled in. One of those areas was the land at the far northern end of the island. Until 1874, the land that was later owned by the Coogan family was underneath the Harlem River. About 15 years later, the new location of the Polo Grounds was on that land, known as Coogan's Hollow. From Coogan's Bluff, the slight promontory to the north of the fields, fans could look down into the hollow and watch games for free, albeit from quite a distance. The Coogans never played polo, as far as we know (though part of the field did see cricket games), but the Polo Grounds name carried forward from the original Bennett usage.

The Players' League lasted only one season, so by 1891, the N.L. Giants had the Polo Grounds all to themselves. Until 1911, this ballpark, with a capacity that varied from about 16,000 to 30,000, depending on improvements, was the home of the New York baseball Giants. (The football version was over a decade from coming into being.) Giants owner John T. Brush (who tried to get people to call the ballpark Brush Stadium to no avail) made numerous additions to attract the high-spending crowd from lower Manhattan to his faraway ballpark at the island's northern tip.

THE MEMORY OF MERKLE

The creation of the American League in 1901 marked the birth of the Major Leagues. The Polo Grounds itself secured its place in baseball history in the 1908 season. That season saw one of the most famous—or infamous, depending on your point of view—gaffes in baseball history. The Giants and Cubs played on September 23 at the Polo Grounds, locked in a tight race for the N.L. pennant. With two outs in the bottom of the ninth of a tie game, Al Bridwell drove in Moose McCormick with the winning run . . . or so thought the crowd that surged and filled the field in celebration. The runner on first, rookie Fred Merkle, saw the mob and sprinted for the clubhouse, located in dead center field. He forgot one thing, but Cubs second baseman Johnny Evers did not: Merkle had not touched second base. Evers retrieved a ball (no one ever knew if it was the one in the game; some accounts have Giants pitcher Joe McGinnity throwing the ball into the crowd), and touched second base, thus

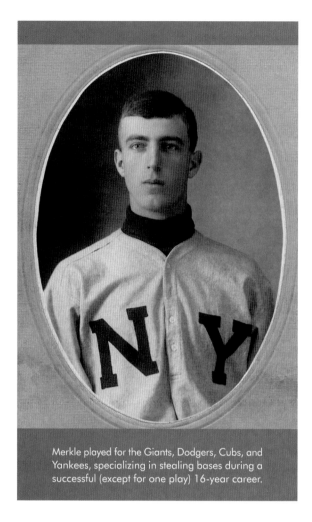

Merkle played for the Giants, Dodgers, Cubs, and Yankees, specializing in stealing bases during a successful (except for one play) 16-year career.

"forcing out" Merkle. The umpires, to many people's amazement, agreed. The run did not count, and since the field was filled with fans, the game was called as a tie. The Cubs appealed to the league president, who ordered the game to be replayed if necessary.

It was. The two teams had identical records after the regular season, so a one-game playoff was necessary. And if you have any sense of drama, you know that poor Merkle took all the blame when the Cubs won that makeup game, played at the Polo Grounds on October 8, 1908, and the pennant. Though he had a fine 16-year career, Merkle's Boner, as it came to be known, remains firmly fixed in baseball's collective memory.

OUT OF THE ASHES

However, this particular Polo Grounds, though home to that and other momentous events, was not as long

Top 10 Moments at the
POLO GROUNDS

(in chronological order)

October 14, 1905

Thanks to the amazing Christy Mathewson and his three shutouts in only six days, the Giants win the World Series over the Philadelphia Athletics.

September 23, 1908

Merkle's Boner; see page 22.

October 8, 1908

The Cubs-Giants playoff game played as a result of the September 23 tie sees the Cubs win 4–2, even though Mathewson started for the Giants.

October 23, 1921

In a best-of-nine World Series, the Giants win in eight games, all of which were played at the Polo Grounds, a World Series first.

October 8, 1922

Déjà vu! Back to best-of-seven, the Giants dispatch their roommates, the Yankees, in five to win back-to-back World Series.

July 10, 1934

At the first All-Star Game held at the Polo Grounds (and only the second ever played), Giants ace Carl Hubbell strikes out five straight future Hall of Famers.

August 1, 1945

Giants legendary slugger Mel Ott, he of the corkscrew batting stance, slugs his 500th home run on his way to a career total of 511.

October 3, 1951

The Miracle of Coogan's Bluff: Bobby Thomson's home run that gives the Giants the N.L. pennant in a playoff with the Dodgers (see page 35).

September 29, 1954

The Catch: Willie Mays of the Giants tracks a mighty blast to deep center field in game 1 of the World Series. His whirling catch-and-throw remains among baseball's most memorable defensive plays.

April 13, 1962

Sure, they were terrible. Yes, they would set a record for losses that hasn't been approached. And Marv Throneberry was their star. But on this day at the Polo Grounds, the New York Mets played the first game of their checkered history.

"Laughin' Larry" Doyle, a Giants second baseman, had the first round-tripper in Polo Grounds history. He played for New York for 13 of his 15 big-league seasons, leading the N.L. in hitting in 1915.

for this world. On April 14, 1911, a fire started in the wooden bleachers that surrounded the lower part of the field. It raged for two days while the Giants were fortunately on the road. When they returned, little was left of their home, which had been made primarily of wood.

Brush wasted no time. He signed a new lease with Mrs. Harriet Coogan and started reconstruction immediately, choosing this time around, however, to use concrete-and-steel construction. In the meantime, the Giants played their early 1911 games at Hilltop Park,

home of the Yankees, a kind of stadium-sharing that would soon be repeated at the Polo Grounds. The firm of Herts and Osborn was hired to design the new structure.

Brush took the opportunity of rebuilding to add some very nice gilding of his baseball lily. The facade around the upper of the two decks sported Roman-inspired friezes. The coats of arms of the National League teams, painted in bright team colors, adorned a wall in the outfield. The clubhouse, located in a building in center field, survived the fire and remained there

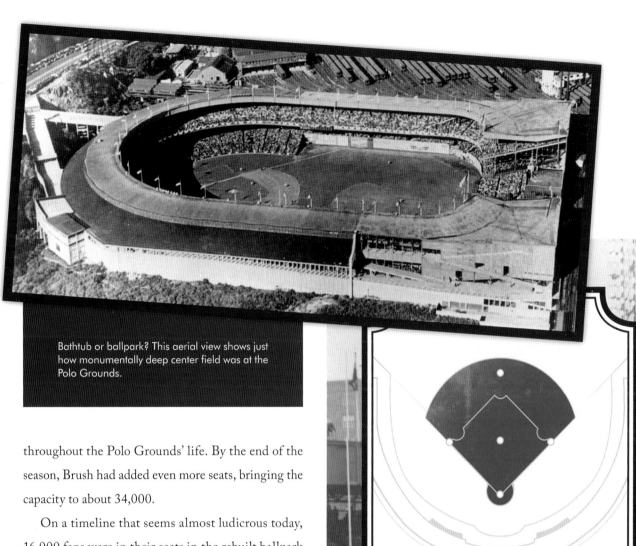

Bathtub or ballpark? This aerial view shows just how monumentally deep center field was at the Polo Grounds.

throughout the Polo Grounds' life. By the end of the season, Brush had added even more seats, bringing the capacity to about 34,000.

On a timeline that seems almost ludicrous today, 16,000 fans were in their seats in the rebuilt ballpark when it opened again for business on June 28, 1911. Just about 10 weeks after the fire, the "new" Polo Grounds was up and running. Christy Mathewson took the hill for the big day, pitching an efficient nine-hit shutout of the Boston Rustlers (later the Braves). Larry Doyle had the first homer in the new ballpark, while Mathewson himself added an RBI sacrifice fly to the 3–0 win.

Meanwhile, the Polo Grounds diamond itself was one of the most unique shapes in the game. While most "classic" diamonds had a pie-shaped arc describing their outfield, the Polo Grounds looked more like a bathtub or a racetrack oval. The distances to the corners of left and right field were each less than 300 feet (277 and 258, respectively), but the distance to dead center field varied over the years from 430 to as much as 505 feet. No one hit homers to dead center unless they were of

Day One

Giants Again at Home

"Home at last after an absence of ten weeks, the Giants won their first game of the season at the spot where they hang their hats, when Mathewson, better known as Matty, shut out the Boston Terriers by a score of 3 to 0 at the partially refurbished Polo Grounds yesterday afternoon."

New York Tribune, June 29, 1911

Between a makeshift barrier and a line of police, fans queued up to get into the 1913 World Series at the Polo Grounds, which the Giants lost to the Athletics.

A group of 1911 Giants, who were part of the N.L. championship that season, stands for a typical publicity picture pose, bats ready.

the inside-the-park variety. The short porches in the corners, however, provided chances for pull hitters to pop a few short flies into the seats. The left field upper deck, in fact, stuck out so far over the playing field that an outfielder could camp under it awaiting a fly ball only to see the ball disappear into the seats above him. The exterior architecture was unremarkable, with none of the flourishes that, for instance, Comiskey Park or Shibe Park were given. Owner John Brush wanted his ballpark to be useful, not fancy.

The playing surface itself, in part to counteract drainage issues caused by the land's former home beneath a river, was sloped and crowned so much that outfielders, from a manager's perspective in the dugout, were but heads and shoulders. The land in right field was even lower, with as much as a two-foot drop from the area behind second base.

CONTENTIOUS COTENANTS

On the field, the Giants were inspired by their newly refurbished surroundings and brought their fans the first of three straight National League pennants in 1911. The first World Series game to be played at the "new" ballpark was on October 14. (The Giants had won the 1905 World Series at the previous incarnation of the Polo Grounds.) New York, behind the pitching of superstar Christy Mathewson, won 2–1. Though the Giants did win another game played at the Polo Grounds, the Philadelphia Athletics came back to win the series in six games.

The Giants repeated the feat of taking the pennant and the disappointment of losing the series in 1912 and 1913. In the 1912 series, they lost in part due to another famous on-field miscue. A tie due to darkness in game 2 meant a deciding eighth game, though played in Boston against the A.L. champion Red Sox. The Giants took a 2-1 lead in the top of the 10th. But in the bottom, New York outfielder Fred Snodgrass dropped an easy fly ball. That opened the door to a Boston comeback and the Red Sox won the series. Snodgrass's Muff, however, joined Merkle's Boner in the Hall of Shame. The Giants lost the series again in 1913, falling again to the Athletics. The Polo Grounds fans had to watch in sadness as the A's celebrated on the Giants' home field after their game 5 victory.

Throughout this run of success, the leader of the Giants on the field was John J. McGraw, one of the most successful, controversial, dictatorial, innovative, and fiery managers the game has ever seen. A star player with the champion Baltimore Orioles in the 1890s, McGraw brought his feisty Irish temper and zeal for victory to the Giants in 1902 and led them for 31 years. McGraw was famous for a win-at-all-costs mentality and a fierce hatred of umpires who did him wrong. He was also a traditionalist who disliked the American League so much that he refused to play the A.L. champs in 1904 in what would have been the second World Series. He relented to play the series, and win, in 1905. In 1906, he then sent the Giants to the field wearing jerseys that declared "World's Champion" instead of "Giants." (As tough as he was, however, he had his soft spots. McGraw got jobs for a couple of his former players, Dan Brouthers and Amos Rusie, at the Polo Grounds. It was apparently not unusual to see the grumpy McGraw huddled with the players-turned-security-guards rehashing old games.)

So McGraw probably was not excited when in 1913 Brush signed a deal to rent the Polo Grounds to the A.L.'s New York Yankees, whose home at Hilltop Field was being torn down. For most of the next decade, from April through September, the Polo Grounds was

John McGraw and another New York managerial legend, little Miller Huggins of the Yankees.

almost never empty of a ball game, as the Giants and Yankees shared the ballpark. A kid with the Red Sox named Babe Ruth hit his first Major League homer at the Polo Grounds in 1915. The sharing reached a fever pitch in 1921 when, for the first time, an entire World Series was played at one ballpark.

Leading the Yankees that year, a hero since joining the club from Boston in 1920, was that man named Ruth. (Perplex your pals by asking how many dingers Ruth hit at Yankee Stadium in his first season with the team: zero.) The powerful left-handed swing of George Herman "Babe" Ruth was tailor-made for the Polo Grounds. (As much as Yankee Stadium's dimensions were later tailored for him, Ruth was reportedly disappointed to leave behind the Polo Grounds, where he hit 32 homers in only 255 at-bats in 1921.) Ruth's

More Than Just THE GIANTS

Baseball:
New York Yankees (A.L.), 1913–1922; New York Cubans (Negro National League), 1948–1950; New York Mets (N.L.), 1962–1964.

Football:
New York Giants, 1925–1955; New York Jets, 1960–1963; college football including Fordham, Army, and Navy.

Soccer:
Numerous games between American teams and international squads, notably the first ever from Israel, were played from the 1920s to the 1950s.

Boxing:
Lots of bouts, but among the biggest were Jack Dempsey vs. Luis Firpo (1923), Joe Louis vs. Billy Conn (1941), and Floyd Patterson vs. Ingemar Johansson (1960).

long-ball exploits, both at the Polo Grounds and on the road, revitalized both the Yankees and baseball. By his second season with the club, he had set yet another single-season home run record (59) and led the Yankees to their first A.L. pennant. Ruth also embarrassed the Giants, as Yankees games in 1921 attracted 350,000 more fans than Giants games.

In that 1921 World Series, McGraw had his revenge on the A.L. Determined not to let his roommates win, he rallied them to a comeback in game 3 that swung the series. The Yankees won the first two games and were ahead in game 3 until a late charge gave the Giants a 13–5 win. The series was best-of-nine that year (the last of a three-season experiment at that length) and the Yanks won three of the first five. But the N.L. club reeled off three straight wins, capping it with a dramatic pitcher's duel that the Giants won 1–0. The fact that an injured Ruth could bat in only five of the eight games helped, and the Giants captured their first championship since 1905 and the first in the rebuilt Polo Grounds.

Except for the lack of batting helmets, this 1921 World Series action could be from last year's series. Ross Youngs hits as Frankie Frisch takes off from first base.

Frankie Frisch, the "Fordham Flash," led the N.L. with 49 stolen bases while also hitting .341 in 1921. It was only the third season of his 19-year Hall of Fame career.

They must have liked the feeling, since they repeated it in 1922. While Giants such as Heinie Groh (.474) and Frankie Frisch (.471) had awesome series stats, Ruth had but two hits in 17 at-bats. For the second year in a row, McGraw rubbed it in the face of his stadium cohorts, this time winning in five games.

ALONE AT LAST

Following the 1922 season, the Yankees moved out and across the river into their new home at Yankee Stadium. Of course, Brush would not take the new Yankee ballpark in stride. Seeing the massive edifice arising across the river (the two ballpark sites are just a few long-distance home runs apart), he added more seats to the Polo Grounds in 1923, enclosing it completely and increasing capacity to more than 54,000.

They needed the extra space soon, since the Giants returned to the World Series in 1923 and 1924. However, in the first of those, it would be their former roomies who took home the big prize. For the first time, the series matched the same pair of teams three years in a row. The two teams alternated games at each ballpark, but the visitors won each of the first four games. McGraw enjoyed spoiling the first World Series game at "the House That Ruth Built," but seethed when Ruth hit a pair of homers at the Polo Grounds to help win game 2.

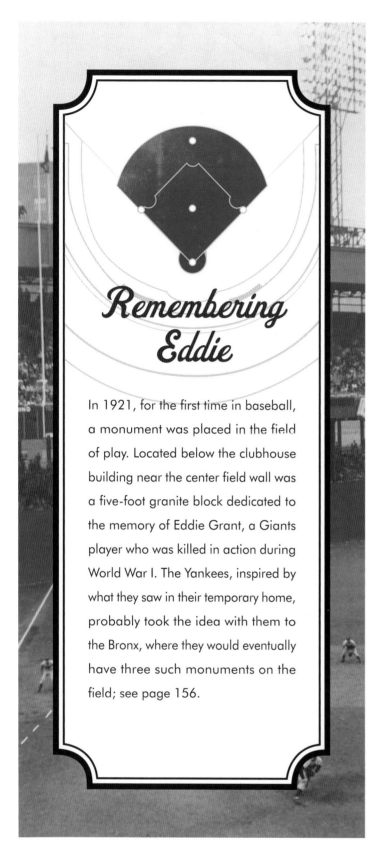

Remembering Eddie

In 1921, for the first time in baseball, a monument was placed in the field of play. Located below the clubhouse building near the center field wall was a five-foot granite block dedicated to the memory of Eddie Grant, a Giants player who was killed in action during World War I. The Yankees, inspired by what they saw in their temporary home, probably took the idea with them to the Bronx, where they would eventually have three such monuments on the field; see page 156.

and then the Giants once again suffered the ignominy of watching another team dance on their own mound when the Yankees won game 6.

In 1924, the Giants made it four N.L. pennants in a row and the Polo Grounds welcomed the World Series back. New York won two of the three played there, but had less luck in Washington against the Senators. In a dramatic game 7, Walter Johnson came out of the bullpen (after winning game 6 just two days earlier) to shut down New York. It was the last World Series for McGraw, though he would lead the team until 1932.

GRIDIRON AND RING

In 1925, the baseball Giants welcomed another cotenant at the Polo Grounds, a team that used balls, but not bats. The New York Giants of the National Football League (yes, they stole the name) played at the Polo Grounds until 1955. The Giants of football, in fact, played host at the Polo Grounds to one of the most memorable games in NFL history in 1934. The championship game came down to the Giants and Chicago Bears. On a frozen field, the game was tied at 3–3 at halftime. However, an alert Giants equipment man dug into the nearby Columbia University gym and returned with sneakers. With better traction on the icy ground, New York dominated play in the second half and won the NFL title in what is still called the "Sneakers Game." The Giants football team also hosted the 1938, 1944, and 1946 NFL title games, winning the first of those.

Football was not the only non-baseball event in those days. In 1923, more than 82,000 people packed the park (seats were set up on the field, too) to watch heavyweight champ Jack Dempsey knock out Luis Firpo. Other big boxing matches were held in that era, when watching live was the only option for any sport and big crowds were still expected at big fights.

Back at Yankee Stadium, Art Nehf pitched a gem for the Giants to win game 3, but the Giants couldn't defend home turf either, losing game 4. The Yankees, behind Bullet Joe Bush, broke the string by winning game 5

A GIANTS TITLE

In 1933, the year after McGraw left, the World Series visited the Polo Grounds again, but this time around former star first baseman Bill Terry was at the helm of the Giants. The opponent was once again the Senators, but this time, it was the Giants who danced on the other team's mound. After winning the first two games at the Polo Grounds, the Giants won two of three in Washington and never had to come back home, snagging the series in the nation's capital.

They were in the series again in 1936, in a rematch of their crosstown rivalry with the Yankees, but the result was different this time. Powered by Joe DiMaggio, the Bronx Bombers won in six. The final game was played at the Polo Grounds, and once again, the Giants watched the winners dance.

The 1940s were not kind to the Giants, as they spent most of the decade in the second division. (Until 1969,

TOP: This view of the 1933 World Series between the Giants and Senators shows Coogan's Bluff still looming behind the ballpark, but the roof now blocked the cheapskates' view.

ABOVE: Giants players enjoy an empty ballpark as they go through warm-ups before a 1934 game.

The helpful dashes show where Thomson's blow flew in 1951, making him, Brooklyn pitcher Ralph Branca, and radio man Russ Hodges famous in baseball forever.

there were only eight teams in each league. Clubs that finished in the bottom half of each league were said to have been in the "second" division, even though there were not actual divisions as there are today.)

One interesting note about this decade: The Polo Grounds got more new tenants but none played ball of any kind. Then-Giants owner Horace Stoneham hated the rival Brooklyn Dodgers. He admired their baseball diamond, however, and conspired to steal the Dodgers' groundskeeper, Matty Schwab. To convince Schwab to jump ship, Stoneham offered up an apartment . . . in the Polo Grounds. Schwab and his family lived in the four-room pad underneath the center field stands until the ball club moved west.

THE SHOT HEARD 'ROUND THE WORLD

After a quiet decade, the Polo Grounds leaped back into the baseball consciousness almost overnight. What happened there in 1951 is still remembered as the Miracle of Coogan's Bluff as well as the Shot Heard 'Round the World.

The Miracle and the Shot were set up by a tight pennant race between the Giants and Dodgers. The Dodgers lost four of the last seven, while the Giants finished with seven straight wins. The Giants tied the Dodgers on the last day of the season, forcing a playoff, which the N.L. decreed to be a three-gamer. The teams split the first two games of that series, setting up game 3 at the Polo Grounds on October 3, 1951, a date that will live in . . . whatever is the opposite of infamy (unless you're a Dodgers fan).

The Dodgers scored three runs in the top of the eighth and held on to that 4–1 lead heading into the bottom of the ninth. Dodgers starting pitcher Don Newcombe struggled to close it out, however. He gave

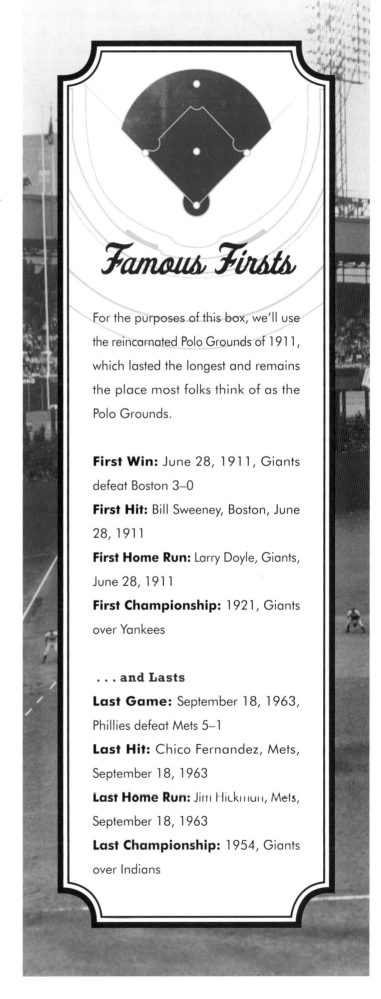

Famous Firsts

For the purposes of this box, we'll use the reincarnated Polo Grounds of 1911, which lasted the longest and remains the place most folks think of as the Polo Grounds.

First Win: June 28, 1911, Giants defeat Boston 3–0
First Hit: Bill Sweeney, Boston, June 28, 1911
First Home Run: Larry Doyle, Giants, June 28, 1911
First Championship: 1921, Giants over Yankees

. . . and Lasts
Last Game: September 18, 1963, Phillies defeat Mets 5–1
Last Hit: Chico Fernandez, Mets, September 18, 1963
Last Home Run: Jim Hickman, Mets, September 18, 1963
Last Championship: 1954, Giants over Indians

ABOVE: What a future this young man has in front of him: Willie Mays was on deck when Thomson slugged his famous homer in 1951.

RIGHT: Thank you, bat, says Thomson, bowing to the wishes of postgame photographers in the celebratory Giants' locker room in 1951.

up consecutive singles before getting an out and then allowing a run-scoring double by Whitey Lockman. That left two on with just one out. Dodgers manager Walter Alston brought in Ralph Branca to pitch to Bobby Thomson, the Giants' left fielder.

On the second pitch, Branca, wearing unlucky No. 13, served up a gopher ball for the ages. Thomson lined the ball into the short porch in left field, a three-run homer that sent the Giants to the World Series. Almost as famous as Thomson's shot and happy jig as he arrived at home was radio man Russ Hodges's ecstatic call: "The Giants win the pennant! The Giants win the pennant! The Giants win the pennant!" Few ballparks have ever

Heroes

The roster of Giants heroes could fill this book, but these key players and managers defined the New York Giants. Years listed are those spent with the Giants.

John McGraw	Player/manager, 1902–1906; manager, 1902–1932
Christy Mathewson	Pitcher, 1900–1916
Frankie Frisch	Infielder, 1919–1926
Mel Ott	Outfielder, 1926–1947
Carl Hubbell	Pitcher, 1928–1943
Willie Mays	Outfielder, 1951–1972

been witness to a more miraculous comeback or a more momentous home run.

Unfortunately, that was all the magic the Giants had that year, as they lost in the World Series to, of course, the Yankees.

THE SAY HEY KID

That '51 season also saw the arrival of the greatest Giants player of all time. Willie Mays, the "Say Hey Kid," jumped into the starting lineup, where he would remain until 1972 (with a year off for military service). Mays would become the team's all-time leader in homers and RBI and just about every other category. He was the Rookie of the Year and later won a pair of MVP awards. Mays earned

24 All-Star selections (though that gets an asterisk; there were two All-Star Games each year from 1959–1962). Along with that, he was one of the best center fielders ever, with a record-tying 12 Gold Gloves. Mays was on deck for Thomson's home run, but he was on center stage for dozens more big events for the Giants.

Perhaps the most famous came three years later in another clutch moment. The Giants had won the 1954 N.L. pennant, but they were big underdogs to the A.L. champion Cleveland Indians. The Tribe had set an A.L. record with 111 wins and looked almost unbeatable. But the Say Hey Kid had something to say about that. In game 1, with the score tied 2–2 in the eighth inning, Cleveland had two men on. Vic Wertz hit a mammoth

Only in the
POLO GROUNDS

- Before 1911, fans could stand 115 feet atop Coogan's Bluff and watch the action on the not-too-distant field.

- The center field clubhouse meant that both teams had to walk the entire length of the field together after the game to reach dressing rooms, which were accessed via long staircases alongside the center field bleachers.

- The massive Longines clock in center field was never dented by a baseball, being more than 500 feet away from home plate and at least 60 feet above the playing field.

- Babe Ruth loved playing here; in 1921, he had 32 homers in only 255 at-bats. Credit his power and the short porch in right field.

drive to the deepest part of the expansive Polo Grounds center field. On a dead run, with his back to the plate, Mays tracked down the ball, caught it, spun immediately, and fired the ball back to hold the runners.

It was stunning. Amazing. Unthinkable. To this day, more than 60 years later, it's considered the greatest catch of all time, especially considering the situation and the player involved. Though Mays said he had made harder ones, this one was and always will be "the Catch." Spurred by the play, the Giants, with the

help of Dusty Rhodes's pinch-hit walk-off homer, won game 1 and went on to fashion a very unlikely sweep of the Indians.

GO WEST, YOUNG MEN

The 1954 series was the last hurrah for the Polo Grounds, however.

Even as the team was celebrating its final championship in New York, plans were beginning to take shape to revolutionize the Major Leagues. Brooklyn

Giants manager Bill Rigney helps workers take some sod from the Polo Grounds to plant in the team's new home, Candlestick Park in San Francisco.

Dodgers owner Walter O'Malley saw a new path for his team, one lined with palm trees and reached after a transcontinental flight. Knowing that he could not move alone, O'Malley met with Stoneham over the ensuing few seasons to convince the Giants owner to move west.

While the entire borough of Brooklyn went into mourning in the fall of 1957 (see Chapter Five), Manhattan traffic didn't stop when the Giants packed up and moved, too. Yes, some fans were upset, but there was little of the emotional, romantic longing attached to the Giants as seemed connected to the Dodgers. How can we tell? There were fewer than 12,000 fans for the Polo Grounds' last game.

The move meant that the Polo Grounds, home of Merkle and McGraw and Mathewson, of Mays and Thomson and Ott, would go dark. After the final game on September 29, 1957, a chunk of sod was dug up and transported to the Giants' new home in Candlestick Park by San Francisco Bay.

MEET THE METS!

Like a baseball game tied after nine, however, the Polo Grounds got some extra innings. First, the American

And down came the walls: In 1964, after the Mets moved out, a baseball-painted wrecking ball, the same ball that had earlier destroyed Ebbets Field, took down the Polo Grounds.

Football League's New York Jets played there from 1960–1963. (Trivia time: In the first three of those seasons, they were actually the New York Titans.) In 1962, another new team, the expansion New York Mets of the National League, was looking for a place to play while their own stadium was built in Queens, and the grand old yard still stood, dusty and weary, on Manhattan's northern tip. A former Giants outfielder, a part of the 1921 and 1922 championship teams, was now the crusty manager of the Mets. Casey Stengel had led the Yankees to 10 World Series as the skipper, a record he would not repeat with the Mets.

In the first of their two seasons at the Polo Grounds, the Mets set an all-time record with 120 losses.

Perhaps that was enough baseball for one place. The Polo Grounds came crashing down for good in spring 1964, while the Giants played in California and the Mets played in Queens. Ironically, the same wrecking ball used to demolish Ebbets Field in 1960 was used to knock down the Polo Grounds too. In the ballpark's place rose a four-building public-housing project named for the home of the Giants.

And that's why, in the mad metropolis that is Manhattan, in the city that never sleeps, you can stay up all night and still not see live Major League Baseball on the island. But once upon a time, after a bit of a subway ride, you could see John McGraw breathe fire, watch Mel Ott uncoil and smite another one, or marvel as Willie Mays's hat came flying off one more time as he covered more ground than a carpet layer. Once upon a time on an island in the east, there used to be a ballpark.

ABOVE: Only the Mets: On Friday the 13th of April, the Mets lined up to play their first game in the Polo Grounds against the Pittsburgh Pirates. They lost.

ENCLOSED 1: An interesting method to sell a set of tickets to the 1911 World Series: The three holes were punched after a fan used this same ticket for three games.

ENCLOSED 2: Announcer Russ Hodges filled out and signed (center right) this Giants scorecard page from the historic October 3, 1951, playoff game.

High above Fenway, this view gives a nice look at how the jigsaw puzzle fits together, with the Mass Pike behind left field. Out of sight at bottom left is Yawkey Way, now the scene of packed humanity before every home game.

CHAPTER THREE

FENWAY PARK

BOSTON, MASS.

YEAR BUILT	1912
HOME TEAM	Boston Red Sox
FIRST GAME	April 20, 1912
CAPACITY (AVERAGE)	38,000
FAMOUS FEATURES	Green Monster left field wall, Citgo ad sign, brick exterior, classic baseball atmosphere

Is it the Green Monster? Is it the hustle and bustle on Yawkey Way outside the ballpark? Is it the Citgo sign and the cozy bullpens and the classic green paint? Is it the lovely brick exterior? Or is it the fact that so much baseball history (and tragedy) has played out on the grass of Fenway Park?

For this humble reporter, it's all that indeed, but it is also—and I say this with the greatest respect for my favorite sports site in the world—the smell. When you pass over your golden ticket and enter, Charlie-like, into the wonderful world of Fenway, the first thing you notice is the century of smell that permeates the place. Fenway Park has been revamped, renovated, upgraded,

TOP: The sign above the gates on Yawkey Way is unchanged from 1912, when Fenway Park opened. The windows now open on to Red Sox team offices.

ABOVE: This view looks down Lansdowne Street, with the famed left field wall at the far right of the picture.

pretzels, and good old-fashioned mustiness. Scientists tell us that smell is our sense most strongly connected to memory; anyone who has smelled Fenway once will know it again instantly a half-century later.

Yankee fans, please insert your "Of course . . . Fenway stinks" joke here, but even jaded New Yawkers join a nation of baseball lovers in agreeing that the "lyric little bandbox," to use John Updike's famous phrase, is the sine qua non of ballparks. Like the Red Sox, Fenway has had its ups and downs, but of late it is very much on the big ups, with a nine-year-long skein of sellouts enjoying a ballpark that masterfully mixes old and new. Fenway is a ballpark, but it is also a palace, a dream destination, a glorious living connection to 100-plus years of baseball in America. Fenway Park is home to the Red Sox, but it belongs to all of baseball.

REAL ESTATE RULES

The most famous ballpark in America (sorry, Wrigley) started out sounding like a line from a con man: Hey,

cleaned, polished, and perfected, but one thing that remains, imbued in the bricks and ensconced in the very beams, is the perfect baseball-park smell. It's not an unpleasant odor, but rather a masterful mélange of old beer, human being, grass, winter, peanuts, steam,

Police on horseback kept a close eye on crowds heading toward the new Fenway Park in 1912, the year it opened.

Boston, I've got some nice swampland I can sell you. On such spurious claims is history made . . . but in this case, it was true. Fenway Park got its name from an area of Boston called the Fens, a word that literally means swamp. Yes, it had been drained years earlier by the good offices of parkland pioneer Frederick Law Olmsted (he of Central Park fame). But even drained, it was still far off the beaten Boston path, sort of a suburb-in-the-making. One man, however, saw gold in them thar Fens, and it was his vision that, a century later, fans enjoy so deeply.

John Taylor had owned the ball club since 1904. But he was also a real estate speculator, and in 1911, he figured out a way to get the most out of both of his investments. As the owner of most of the land in the restored Fenway area, he "sold" himself a large plot around Lansdowne Street and Jersey Street. He then sold half of the ball club to a pair of baseball men from Washington, Jimmy McAleer and Robert McRoy. Taylor then built and rented to the Red Sox the ballpark we enjoy today. Yes, he made out like a bandit on the swap, but good for him and us.

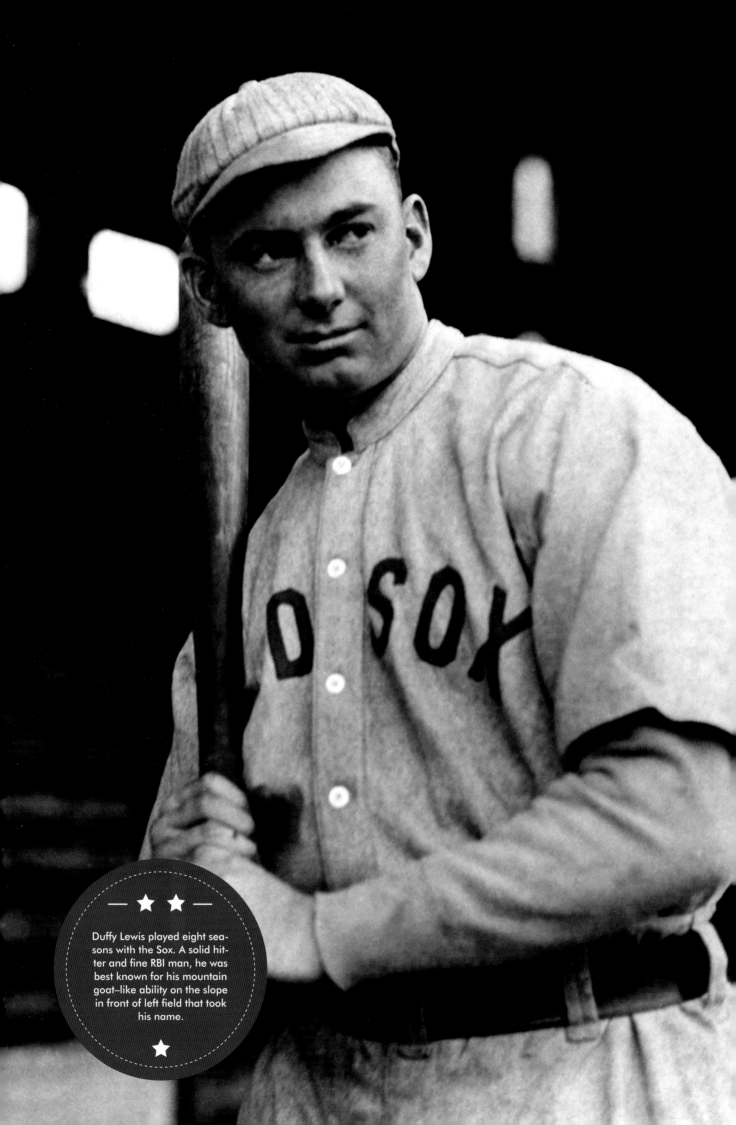

Duffy Lewis played eight seasons with the Sox. A solid hitter and fine RBI man, he was best known for his mountain goat–like ability on the slope in front of left field that took his name.

A key part of the success of the location, then considered far from Boston's main downtown, was convincing city fathers to extend the trolley line to nearby Kenmore Square. So when today's fans step off the green T trains and emerge in the square to walk across the bridge over the Mass Pike, they can thank Mr. Taylor for their ride.

As for the actual building itself, designer James McLaughlin and builder Osborn Engineering had to contend with some pretty funky street shapes that outlined the plot. Having to fill the entire city block meant that Fenway's original center field was nearly 500 feet away from home. Left field, however, was considerably closer, perhaps 320 feet, while the right field corner dipped in 314 feet. The single deck of seats was built with the new concrete-and-steel type of construction, ensuring solidity, though outfield pavilions were wooden still. The exterior was brick and its lovely "tapestry" pattern remains a signature part of the look of the ballpark.

Construction started in September 1911 and continued right up until the scheduled opening day of April 17, 1912. Opening day was delayed by rain, unfortunately, muting the tenor of the ceremonies, which were finally held three days later, on April 20, 1912. Further muting the mood was the same-day news of the sinking of the *Titanic*. As other thoughtful writers have noted, on the day the unsinkable liner went down, another unbeatable edifice opened in a kind of monumental reincarnation. The Red Sox treated fans to a pretty good game, coming from behind in 11 innings to beat the Yankees, 7–6.

Fenway in those days did sport a high wall in left field, but it was nothing like the Green Monster that lives there today . . . about which more anon. Instead, its most distinguishing playing-field feature took its name from the team's outstanding left fielder. Duffy Lewis was a master of running up the small incline that

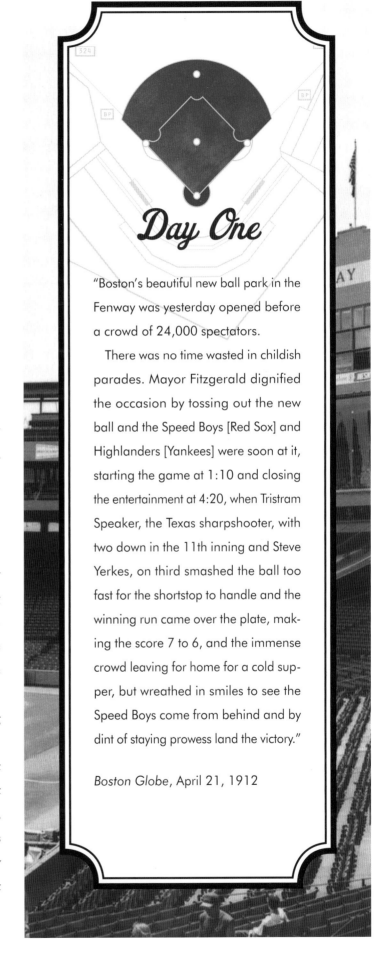

Day One

"Boston's beautiful new ball park in the Fenway was yesterday opened before a crowd of 24,000 spectators.

There was no time wasted in childish parades. Mayor Fitzgerald dignified the occasion by tossing out the new ball and the Speed Boys [Red Sox] and Highlanders [Yankees] were soon at it, starting the game at 1:10 and closing the entertainment at 4:20, when Tristram Speaker, the Texas sharpshooter, with two down in the 11th inning and Steve Yerkes, on third smashed the ball too fast for the shortstop to handle and the winning run came over the plate, making the score 7 to 6, and the immense crowd leaving for home for a cold supper, but wreathed in smiles to see the Speed Boys come from behind and by dint of staying prowess land the victory."

Boston Globe, April 21, 1912

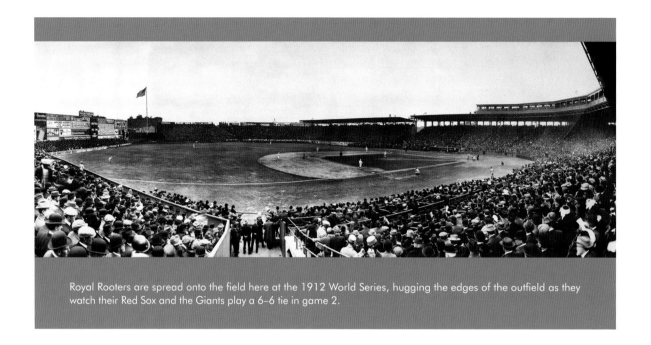

Royal Rooters are spread onto the field here at the 1912 World Series, hugging the edges of the outfield as they watch their Red Sox and the Giants play a 6–6 tie in game 2.

was built at the base of the left field wall. It was there to act as reserve bleachers for busy days at the park; fans would be escorted there to stand en masse like a Greek chorus at the base of the wall. When it was not filled with fans, however, "Duffy's Cliff" was Lewis's playground and he routinely ran up or down it to make spectacular catches.

Lewis was part of one of the best outfields ever in baseball, joined by Harry Hooper and Tris Speaker. Together, along with a pitching staff led by Smokey Joe Wood, they led Boston to the A.L. pennant in its first season in Fenway Park. As hosts of the World Series, they were happy to have their new ballpark to pack with fans. Some of those fans, in fact, were as well known as the players, but a seating mix-up nearly caused a riot.

GLORY AND A CURSE

The first World Series game in Fenway Park history did not yield a winner. Instead, the New York Giants and the Red Sox played to a 6–6, 11-inning tie that was called by darkness. Later, Boston led three games to two and needed just one win to capture the title. Fenway got an extra game due to the tie, but the team neglected to set aside seats at that game for the Royal Rooters. Led

by the saloonkeeper Ned "Nuf Said" McGreevey, the Royal Rooters were the ultimate fan club, attendees at every game in their usual seats in left field, marching out en masse before each game to the playing of a band and the cheers of thousands. However, for this game 7, they found their seats occupied. A near-riot ensued with crowds of Rooters battling regular fans, police, and club officials. They even knocked down an outside fence in the scuffle. Finally, order was restored, but the great Wood, 34–5 on the season, didn't make it to the second inning. It took a stirring game 8 tenth-inning comeback to give Boston its first title since 1903.

It was the start of a tremendous run for the Olde Towne Team, as they played in three more World Series in the decade, winning again in 1915, 1916, and 1918. The 1914 World Series was also played at Fenway Park, as the N.L.'s Boston Braves needed a place larger than their own dumpy grounds. The park must have still had some magic, because the "Miracle Braves" swept the Athletics to complete their amazing comeback—they had been in last place in late July. Oddly, in the 1915 World Series, the Red Sox played in the Braves' new home, packing in more than 40,000 fans, twice Fenway's capacity at the time.

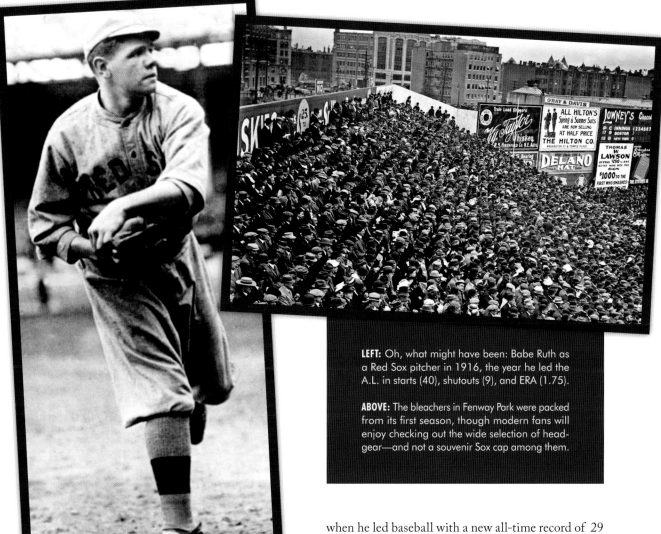

LEFT: Oh, what might have been: Babe Ruth as a Red Sox pitcher in 1916, the year he led the A.L. in starts (40), shutouts (9), and ERA (1.75).

ABOVE: The bleachers in Fenway Park were packed from its first season, though modern fans will enjoy checking out the wide selection of head-gear—and not a souvenir Sox cap among them.

For the 1916 and 1918 series, Boston welcomed a new pitching hero whose career would play a huge part in Red Sox history, though mostly for the wrong reasons. Boston signed Babe Ruth from Baltimore in 1914, and he joined the team for good in 1915. He won at least 18 games as a dandy left-handed pitcher every year from 1915 to 1917 and led the A.L. with a 1.75 ERA in 1916. His World Series record of 29.2 consecutive scoreless innings stood for 43 years. He was 2–0 in the 1918 World Series, the last that Boston would win in the 20th century.

In his final season with Boston, Ruth, though still a winning pitcher, showed serious signs of his true calling when he led baseball with a new all-time record of 29 homers. The confluence of events that would deeply affect Boston was coming to a head in the team offices on Lansdowne Street. With Ruth suddenly even more valuable than before and with a need to raise money for non-baseball ventures, including Broadway shows, owner Harry Frazee—and this hurts even now to write this, nearly a century after the fact—sold Ruth to the Yankees for the 1920 season. He also gave the Yanks a mortgage on Fenway Park itself.

The Curse of the Bambino was born. Frazee's Folly cast the team into the doldrums for the next 20 years and kept it out—or so the soothsayers say—of the ultimate winner's circle for nearly a century. While the Yankees rose to the top on Ruth's back and bat, the Sox sank back into the fens. Fenway Park itself didn't fare much better, as new owner Bob Quinn let the ballpark fall

Only in
FENWAY PARK

★ ★ ★

- The left field scoreboard, still hand-operated, has the initials of Mr. and Mrs. Tom Yawkey in Morse code between sections.

- The ladder on the left field wall was in use until the Monster seats were added, and the roll-up door in the left field corner is still in play.

- A statue of Ted Williams stands outside the right field wall, while another honors "the Teammates": Williams, Bobby Doerr, Dom DiMaggio, and Johnny Pesky.

---

to near-ruin, not even rebuilding parts of the stands after a 1926 fire. By 1932, the team had reached a new low in both wins and attendance. But as would prove to be the case over the ensuing decades, Fenway Park was resilient. And along came a savior just when one was needed.

YAWKEY'S WAY

Tom Yawkey's long tenure as owner of the Red Sox had a surprising beginning and a disappointing ending. At the start, he was an unknown rich kid, just turned 30, who wanted a baseball team to play with. At the end, he was an old man whose sole dream in life—a World Series title—never came true. However, for the Red Sox and Fenway Park, he came along at just the right moment to turns things around. After buying the team from Quinn before the 1933 season, Yawkey immediately started spending like a junior George Steinbrenner, dropping nearly a quarter-million dollars adding players. This was the height of the Depression, remember, and fans were both shocked and thrilled.

They were even more excited when Yawkey announced an almost complete rebuilding of Fenway Park. New concrete seating would replace the wooden forms in right field, box seats were added all around (with home plate moving closer to center field), and a big scoreboard was set for the wall in left. Capacity would increase to nearly 38,000. He spent $1.5 million, not really a drop from his capacious bucket, thanks to inheriting wealth repeatedly. As the authors of *Red Sox Century*

The 1933 rebuilding of Fenway Park probably looked a lot like this scene of the building of the first walls in 1912. The old yard was heavily refurbished by new owner Tom Yawkey.

also pointed out, the massive construction site "was like Yawkey's own private WPA project, and turned hundreds of workers and their families into Red Sox fans."

Yawkey's crews had to work around another sport to get his "new" ballpark built. The NFL's Boston Redskins were playing their first season at Fenway in late 1933; they would share the place with the Sox until 1936. (Worth noting here that another NFL team played in Fenway from 1944 to 1948, but perhaps it was their choice of moniker that doomed them to a succession of losing seasons: the Yanks.)

Football season over, the construction roared ahead. Unfortunately, a fire on January 5, 1934, destroyed the incomplete center field bleachers. Amazingly, working double shifts, construction crews still finished the renovations. The many now-familiar angles and vistas of Fenway Park came into being with this renovation,

including painting of much of the park in what was then called Dartmouth green. The scoreboard on the left field wall still used today was installed then, too—the first to use electric lights to record balls and strikes. Towering above it were massive advertising signs, so dominant in their space that it was a wonder players were not distracted. One was for Calvert beer, another for Gem razor blades, and later Lifebuoy soap.

Tom Yawkey had proven to be Fenway Park's savior. In 1939, however, another savior arrived, this time a man who would define the team and baseball greatness for two decades.

The slim form of the Splendid Splinter shows how Ted Williams earned one of his many nicknames. He's shown here in 1941 when he hit a stirring .406.

TEDDY BALLGAME

A long, tall drink of water from San Diego showed up in Boston with a bat and a chip on his skinny shoulders. Ted Williams was not shy about anything, least of all his own opinions about his hitting ability. But as they say, it's not bragging if you back it up, and the young man who claimed he would be the "greatest hitter who ever lived" did little to help arguments against. He set

a rookie record with 145 RBI in 1939. He hit .327 as a rookie, then .340 in his second season, the first of 11 seasons he would spend above that mark. He could club it, too, leading the A.L. four times in homers. Williams, in fact, joins Rogers Hornsby as the only players ever to earn the Triple Crown twice (1942 and 1947).

Toward the end of Williams's debut season in '39, Yawkey announced a change in Fenway designed to take

Top 10 Moments at
FENWAY PARK

(in chronological order)

September 11, 1918
The Sox beat the Cubs in the World Series, Boston's last title in the 20th century.

October 9, 1946
Behind "Boo" Ferriss, the Sox win their first home World Series game since 1918, beating the Cardinals 4–0.

September 28, 1960
In his final career at-bat, Ted Williams hits a home run at Fenway Park. He does not tip his cap.

October 1, 1967
The Red Sox cap their "Impossible Dream" summer with a pennant-clinching win over the Twins.

October 21, 1975
Carlton Fisk's homer in the bottom of the 12th ends one of the greatest World Series games ever with a win.

October 1, 1983
On Yaz Day, Fenway honors one of its greatest heroes on his retirement.

April 29, 1986
Roger Clemens sets a Major League record by striking out 20 Seattle Mariners in nine innings.

July 13, 1999
In the All-Star Game, Pedro Martinez is the MVP and Ted Williams is honored as part of the All-Century Team announced at the game.

October 17, 2004
In game 4 of the ALCS, a ninth-inning steal by Dave Roberts leads to a come-from-behind win over the Yankees. The Sox go on to win their next eight games and their first World Series in 86 years.

October 30, 2004
As part of the Red Sox victory parade, the World Series trophy rides into Fenway for the first time in 86 years.

The bullpens were moved in front of the right field wall and renamed Williamsburg, in an effort to take advantage of the hot-hitting lefty.

advantage of the young slugger's power. The bullpens were moved from the edges of the field to the back of right field, in front of the right field stands. The distance a Williams homer would have to travel shrunk from 402 to 380, while the corner pole was now just 302 feet away. A dead-pull hitter, "the Kid" could take aim at the bullpens. Oddly, even with the new "Williamsburg," as the pens were called, Teddy Ballgame hit 23 homers in his second year, down from 31 in his first.

In 1941, Williams became the last player in baseball history to top .400 for a season, finishing at .406. The next season, however, he, along with many big leaguers, joined the military during World War II. Williams actually became a fighter pilot and served again in the Korean War. What would his numbers

have been had he not given up nearly five full seasons to his country?

One good outcome of the war years was the arrival of perhaps the Red Sox's most loyal fan. Elizabeth "Lib" Dooley was a regular at Fenway from 1944 to the day she died in 2000. Along with being president of a team booster club in the 1950s, she became a good friend to generations of players, from Williams to Yaz to Jim Rice. (Her father, John S. Dooley, who had helped start the ball club in 1901, reputedly also didn't miss a home opener from 1894 to 1970, according to the *Boston Globe*.) Another earlier famous fan was Lillian "Lolly" Hopkins, who earned her lifetime pass while heading to Fenway from 1932 to 1959. Her devotion was such that she was featured at the Baseball Hall of Fame in

a display of famous fans. Red Sox Nation would come to be comprised of such loyalty.

Williams returned in 1946 and gave Dooley and the other Fenway Faithful a handful of memories. First, on June 9, Williams hit a homer that is still marked in Fenway with a special red seat far off in the green sea of the right field bleachers. The clout off Fred Hutchinson of the Tigers flew more than 500 feet, landing on the noggin and breaking the straw hat of one Joseph Boucher. During a 1984 renovation, team owners memorialized the feat by posting the red seat where the ball landed (section 42, row 31, seat 21, since you asked).

A month later, during the All-Star Game, Williams patiently waited for Rip Sewell's famous "eephus" lob pitch to come down and promptly clobbered it into Williamsburg. The blow highlighted a 12–0 A.L. rout. He had actually swung and missed at the first such offering, taken a second, and then whacked the third.

By October, he had led the team to the World Series for the first time since 1918. The opponent was the St. Louis Cardinals, and Boston gave them all they could handle. The series went seven games, including two Sox victories in Fenway, but the Cardinals won at home in game 7 as Enos Slaughter raced home in the bottom of the eighth with the winning run. Did he score from first on a single? Did shortstop Johnny Pesky hold the ball too long, as most people still recall the event? The facts say "sort of" and the myth says yes, but had his relay throw been on line (he only hesitated a fraction of a second, surprised to see Slaughter heading home), it's a different ball game.

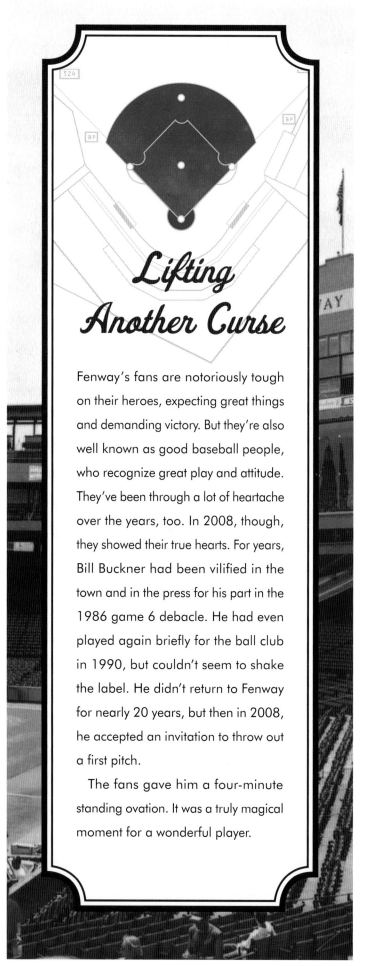

Lifting Another Curse

Fenway's fans are notoriously tough on their heroes, expecting great things and demanding victory. But they're also well known as good baseball people, who recognize great play and attitude. They've been through a lot of heartache over the years, too. In 2008, though, they showed their true hearts. For years, Bill Buckner had been vilified in the town and in the press for his part in the 1986 game 6 debacle. He had even played again briefly for the ball club in 1990, but couldn't seem to shake the label. He didn't return to Fenway for nearly 20 years, but then in 2008, he accepted an invitation to throw out a first pitch.

The fans gave him a four-minute standing ovation. It was a truly magical moment for a wonderful player.

THE MONSTER RISES

Not long after that World Series disappointment, another Boston legend was born, but this one a much happier one. The high left field wall had long been the park's signature architectural note, but it was usually covered with ads. In 1947, it was painted Dartmouth green to match the rest of the ballpark (it's now officially painted a trademarked and private brand called "Fence Green," made by California Paints of Andover, Massachusetts). The Green Monster was born, though the nickname wouldn't catch on for decades. Standing 37 feet, 2 inches tall, it sported a massive 23-foot screen atop it to prevent baseballs from hitting buildings and cars behind it. As we'll see, in 2003, the Sox came up with a better idea than a giant screen.

But the Monster would always play a big part in the histories of both Fenway and the Sox. The team for years tilted toward right-handed power hitters who could bang baseballs off the tin plates. And yet, paradoxically, its two greatest hitters, Williams and Carl Yastrzemski, were both lefties. On defense, having hometowners who could play the caroms off the wall gave the Sox a big advantage. Williams was fine, but Yaz turned it into an art form. He won seven Gold Gloves and led the A.L. in assists seven times. His best move was to stand almost still as a ball soared over his head, fooling the batter into thinking it was headed over the Monster. A home run trot might end suddenly at second base after Yaz played in the carom. Left field offers another fielding quirk due to the closeness of the stands jutting toward the foul line past third base. A fair ball pulled down the line might bounce to the right back onto the field. Shortstops for generations know to head to short left on a ball pulled past third.

Towering above the wall, outside the ballpark, is a massive sign for Citgo gas that has stood since 1940.

WORLD
SERIES
CHAMPIONS

20
YAWKEY WAY
CLUB ENTRANCE

GATE
A

★ ★

Originally Jersey Street, Yawkey
Way was renamed in honor of the
longtime Sox owner Tom Yawkey.
INSET: Before the Monster seats,
there was simply the Monster,
looming in left field to taunt right-
handed hitters.

★

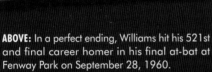

ABOVE: In a perfect ending, Williams hit his 521st and final career homer in his final at-bat at Fenway Park on September 28, 1960.

RIGHT: This is the face of "the Kid" and "Teddy Ballgame," a man who by any name was the greatest hitter in Red Sox history, and perhaps in baseball's too.

At first it was a big green shamrock, but in 1965, Citgo lit up the now-familiar red triangle. Since then, the Citgo sign has been the guiding light for fans around the ballpark. It was also the easiest way to locate the park from a distance, flashing red and white through the night. Citgo is now owned by the Venezuelan government, but the sign is so much a part of Boston's skyline that its landmarks commission makes sure it stays. It's now lit by more than 200,000 weather-resistant LEDs.

Another sign with a long history at Fenway is for the Jimmy Fund, founded a year after the Monster was painted green. The Red Sox adopted the local charity, which helps kids with cancer through the Dana Farber Institute. The fund uses Jimmy, a pseudonym for a young patient, as the symbol. Over the years, the Sox have helped raise more than $750 million for the fund. From its first days, one of the biggest boosters was the man they called "the Kid," Williams. Without fanfare or press, he was a regular visitor with the kids in local hospitals. Few teams are as connected with a cause as the Sox are with the Jimmy Fund.

TEDDY'S LAST BALL GAME

By 1950, the Red Sox boasted one of the most potent offenses ever, setting A.L. records for runs and homers (later broken), led by Williams but aided by names like Vern Stephens, Walt Dropo, and Dom DiMaggio. But as would prove the case for the next decade-plus, poor pitching doomed the Sox. The 1950s were a fairly quiet decade, but they ended with yet another magical moment from Ted Williams.

From the start of his career, the thin-skinned slugger hated the catcalls and criticism from the fans. He

Playing
FENWAY
★ ★ ★

Fans in Yankee Stadium enjoy Frank Sinatra after Yankees wins, but Red Sox fans enjoy a host of musical traditions. Here are three of the most well known:

- The Royal Rooters of the early 1900s sang a lot of songs, but "Tessie," from a popular musical of the day and easily transformed to mock opponents, was a favorite. During the Sox run in 2004, a rockin' version of the song blared constantly.

- In the middle of the eighth inning, Sox fans sing along to Neil Diamond's "Sweet Caroline." Why, you ask? Why not?

- Another tradition started around 2004 as a song mentioning Boston was heard following Sox wins: "Dirty Water" by the Standells. "Ohhhh, Boston, you're my home!"

and they had a prickly relationship, as he took every slight personally, and they enjoyed slighting him, as much for his reaction as anything else. In response, he refused to tip his cap after a homer or in response to applause. On September 28, 1960, in what he had announced would be his final home game (and would turn out to be his final game ever), in his last at-bat in Fenway Park, Williams smacked a home run to right field. He rounded the bases, head down, and went into the dugout, never to return as a player. This was the occasion of John Updike's famous ode to both player and place in the *New Yorker*, "Hub Fans Bid Kid Adieu." And so, we do, too.

THE IMPOSSIBLE DREAM

Though now it is beloved and nearly untouchable, Fenway did not always capture the hearts of fans as it does today. By 1967, Boston fans were watching new

More Than Just
THE RED SOX

Baseball:

Lots of local college and high school tournaments; Homestead Greys exhibition, May 1944

Football:

Boston Redskins (NFL), 1933–1936; Boston Yanks (NFL), 1944–1948; Boston Patriots (AFL), 1963–1968; many college games including the annual Holy Cross–Boston College clash

Basketball:

Harlem Globetrotters, July 29, 1954

Soccer:

Boston Beacons (NASL), 1968; Sporting vs. Celtic friendly, 2010

Boxing:

Numerous fights, mostly among local boxers

Hurling:

Played as part of an Irish sports field day in 1914

"modern" ballparks arise, with others on the drawing board, and even Fenway was threatened. Their team was pretty lousy, enjoying an eight-year string of second-division finishes. Yastrzemski had replaced Williams in patrolling left field, and though he was an All-Star and a batting champ by then, the team barely cracked fifth place.

And then came 1967. Perhaps more than any other season, that one year saved Fenway and began its march to the exalted position it holds for fans today. The team's

"Impossible Dream" pennant cemented the love of a generation of New England fans and made Fenway Park the epicenter of that love.

As the team hovered at or around the top of the league, the entire region seemed to come alive. Fans who went through it said that it became a shared thrill ride as Yaz, pitching ace Jim Lonborg, and the other Sox gamely kept winning, as much with guts and guile as overwhelming talent. In 1966, attendance at Fenway was less than a million. In 1967, it more than doubled

and has never been less than 1.4 million in a full season since. For the team and ballpark, this was the turnaround season. Suddenly, the Red Sox mattered again. In Yaz, they found a blue-collar hero to rally around, and he paid them off in spades. On the last days of the regular season, needing to beat the Twins twice, Yaz was seven for eight with a homer. He wrapped up a Triple Crown season, the last one ever in the majors (through 2012). Though Boston lost the series in seven to a powerful Cardinals team, just winning the pennant was almost enough. The image of Lonborg being carried off the field, his shirt in tatters, is almost like Fenway's rebirth announcement. The magic was back.

If the Impossible Dream of 1967 (which took its name from the contemporaneous musical *Man of La Mancha*) gave Fenway the magic, seven years later another epochal event used some of it up. The Red Sox were again in the World Series, this time on the backs of two of the best rookies ever, outfielders Jim Rice and Fred Lynn. In game 6 against the Reds, they gave the Fenway fans what is still regarded as one of the best, if not the greatest, World Series games ever. A back-and-forth clash with the Reds went to extra innings, with each team having victory snatched away by the other. Finally, leading off the 12th, catcher Carlton Fisk pulled a low pitch toward the Green Monster and the looming foul pole. Urged by 35,000 screaming fans and one arm-waving batter,

MAJOR LEAGUE BASEBALL® OFFICIAL PROGRAM $10

BOSTON
ALL★STAR
GAME '99
™

1999

TOP: How the area above home plate looked before the major renovation that created a luxury-box section. **RIGHT:** The official program for the 1999 All-Star Game, a memorable celebration of baseball in the 20th century.

Heroes

★ ★ ★

The list of Red Sox heroes could fill (and has filled) books galore. Here are just a few of the Fenway favorites through the years. The years listed are those that the player spent with Boston.

Babe Ruth	Pitcher/outfielder, 1914–1919
Ted Williams	Outfielder, 1939–1960
Carl Yastrzemski	Outfielder, 1960–1983
Dwight Evans	Outfielder, 1972–1991
Jim Rice	Outfielder, 1974–1989
Roger Clemens	Pitcher, 1984–1996
Pedro Martinez	Pitcher, 1998–2004
Manny Ramirez	Outfielder, 2001–2008

the ball just stayed fair, giving the Sox an epic win and Fisk's wave a place in baseball history.

Sadly, they then lost game 7 after leading 3–0.

A few years later, the team wrapped up another era with Yaz Day, October 1, 1983. He was not the first big star to get a day, but he was the first to really revel in it. As the last out was made and he came out for final bows, he began to jog slowly around the edge of the Fenway Park field, touching outstretched hands, waving, and basking in the cheers and his last moments on a field where he had given so much.

FENWAY SURVIVES . . . AND THRIVES

Three years later, the Sox were in the World Series again and the only good thing to say about that event from a Boston perspective is that their inglorious end did not happen at Fenway Park. Boston had left the Fens up three games to two over the Mets and needing one win to capture their first World Series since 1918. But as any baseball fan knows, the team managed to choke away a lead in the 10th inning of game 6, allowing the winning run as first baseman Bill Buckner misplayed a ground ball. Billy Bucks was a terrific player wrongly

Inspiring Baltimore

In the early 1990s, Larry Lucchino was planning to build a new ballpark in Baltimore, a structure that would become Oriole Park at Camden Yards. For inspiration and guidance, he looked north—to Fenway Park. Oriole Park's combination of classic features, decorative ironwork, brick walls, and incorporating the shape of the park with the city blocks around it? All inspired by Fenway.

Oriole Park, which opened in 1992, started a whole new round of ballpark construction. And while the new parks in the 1960s and 1970s had mostly been multipurpose places with (gasp) artificial turf, the new parks for the new millennium all harked back to the original jewel boxes (though with luxury suites, wireless access, and more bathrooms). The train that runs around the edge of Minute Maid in Houston, the jutting right field stands in Arlington, the downtown feel of the Indians' home—all pay homage in one way or another to the ballparks in this book.

saddled with goat horns; as in 1975, the Sox led in game 7 but blew that, too.

As the team was being revived after the pain of '86, the team's owners and Boston considered various schemes to replace Fenway Park. It had become old and crunchy, too much so in a time when salaries were rising and owners needed dough. It was not the first time that such scandalous (to many fans) plans had been foisted. There was a big dome in the late 1960s, a late-1980s replacement park, and a $300 million plan for a building right next door. None of these came to

fruition, and then in 1999, baseball held an event that cemented Fenway in baseball's collective consciousness.

Celebrating the end of the 20th century, Major League Baseball, with help from fans and experts, chose its All-Century Team, which was unveiled at the All-Star Game. And they held the game at Fenway Park. It was perfect. A salute to all that was good and great about the game at a place where so much good and great had happened and that retained such a distinct flavor of the game's origins. Capping off the roll call of great players, many of whom were there in person, from Stan Musial

Now among the most coveted and unique seats in baseball, the Monster seats loom above left field, high atop Fenway's Green Monster.

and Willie Mays to Nolan Ryan and Bob Gibson, was the appearance, in a golf cart, of the Thumper himself, Teddy Ballgame, the Splendid Splinter.

Williams rolled in to endless cheers and was quickly surrounded by players ancient and current. It was a celebration of the game and its players, but it gave Fenway an enduring and unbeatable shine as one of the game's great shrines.

Four years later, another miracle: The park and the team were bought by John Henry and Tom Werner, who vowed to not only keep Fenway, but to make it

better than ever. One of their first moves was to install seats atop the left field wall. The Monster seats quickly became baseball's hottest ticket and nine years later sell out every game, including standing-room spots for $60 a pop. Over the ensuing years, the owners have added a few seats here and there, cleaned out some of the clutter, sharpened up the public areas, and polished it until it shines. They have done a marvelous job of paying attention to history (the luxury seats above home plate are the 406 Club—get it?) while also bringing the ballpark into the 21st century.

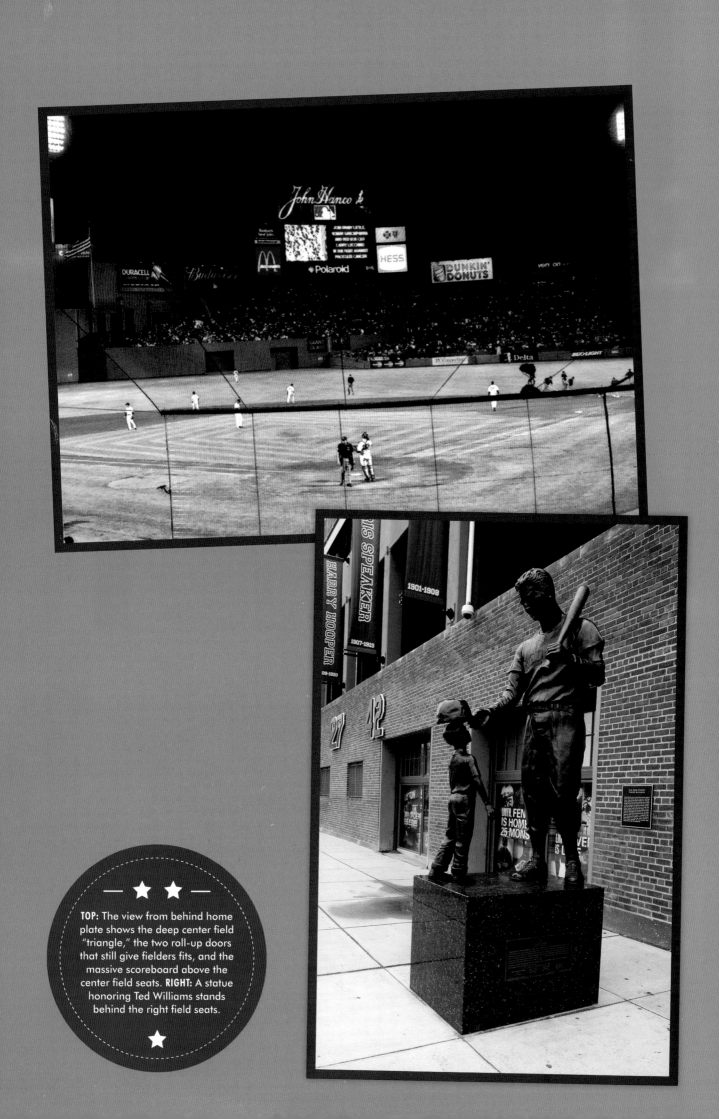

THE CURSE IS LIFTED

Of all the magic and miracles that Fenway has seen, from Ruth to Teddy Ballgame to the Impossible Dream and Fisk's wave, none could match a few days in October 2004 for sheer, mad brilliance. And it all started at Fenway on October 17. The Red Sox trailed their archenemies, the Yankees, three games to none. They trailed in game 4 at 4–3, just three outs from watching the Bombers dance on their graves again.

Then Dave Roberts stole second.

To Red Sox fans, those words kick off a cascade of memories as hardwired as our children's birthdays. In short order, or so it felt, Roberts scored, the game was tied, Boston won in extra innings. They repeated the feat at Fenway the next night. They won two more in Yankee Stadium. Almost suddenly, they had completed the greatest comeback in baseball history, the only team ever to come back from being three games down to win a postseason series.

After their stunning comeback, the Sox still had to finally "Reverse the Curse" in the World Series. games 1 and 2 against the St. Louis Cardinals were at Fenway. The Sox won game 1, then sent pitcher Curt Schilling to the mound for game 2. His injured ankle had been temporarily repaired, and during the game the stitches popped, soaking his sock with blood, an almost ritualistic capper to this stunning season. Boston won game 2 and swept games 3 and 4 in St. Louis almost as an afterthought. And they were champs, for the first time in 86 years.

The Curse of the Bambino was lifted forever. The only way it could have been sweeter would have been to have it play out on Fenway's hallowed greensward. No matter—the team staged a massive victory parade, including a lap around the park, through Boston, and down the Charles River, that was seen by as many as two

Famous Firsts

First Win: April 20, 1912, Red Sox defeat Yankees 7–6

First Hit: Steve Yerkes, Red Sox, April 20, 1912

First Home Run: Hugh Bradley, Red Sox, April 26, 1912

First Championship: 1912, Red Sox over Giants

million people. And reverberating through the whole thing was a song called "Tessie," first sung on Fenway's opening day in 1912 by the Royal Rooters and revamped and revived by local heroes the Dropkick Murphys in a perfect circle back to connect past and present.

Get rid of Fenway? You might as well tear down the Old North Church.

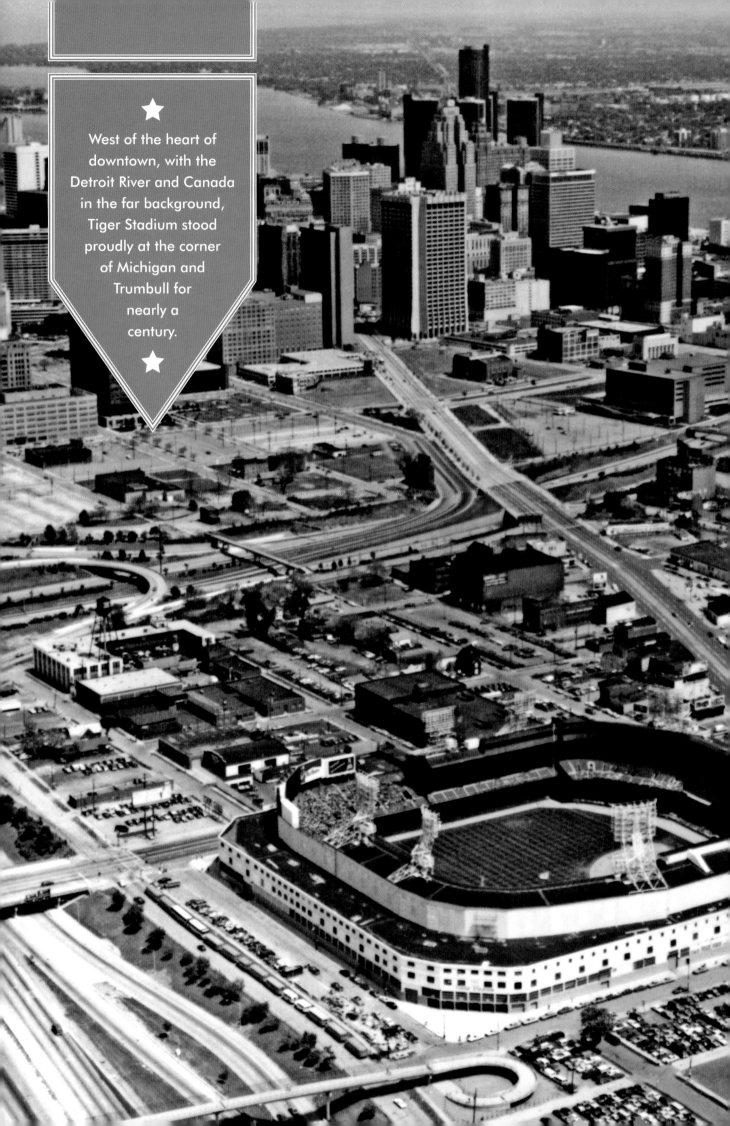

West of the heart of downtown, with the Detroit River and Canada in the far background, Tiger Stadium stood proudly at the corner of Michigan and Trumbull for nearly a century.

CHAPTER FOUR

TIGER STADIUM

DETROIT, MICH.

YEAR BUILT	1912
HOME TEAM	Detroit Tigers
FIRST GAME	April 20, 1912
LAST GAME	September 27, 1999
CAPACITY (AVERAGE)	52,000
FAMOUS FEATURES	Overhanging deck in right field, flagpole in center field, downtown Detroit neighborhood

Most baseball fans can identify what team plays on Yawkey Way. The address of 1060 W. Addison is well known enough to have been used in the *Blues Brothers* movie. And even though it's not in our book, Chavez Ravine is a famed baseball address.

The intersection of Michigan and Trumbull, known to locals in Detroit simply as "the Corner," might not be as recognizable. But that fabled intersection was home to big-league baseball in the Motor City for more than a century. Today, it's just a well-preserved field to which a group of diehards cling while trying to keep the magic of Tiger Stadium alive.

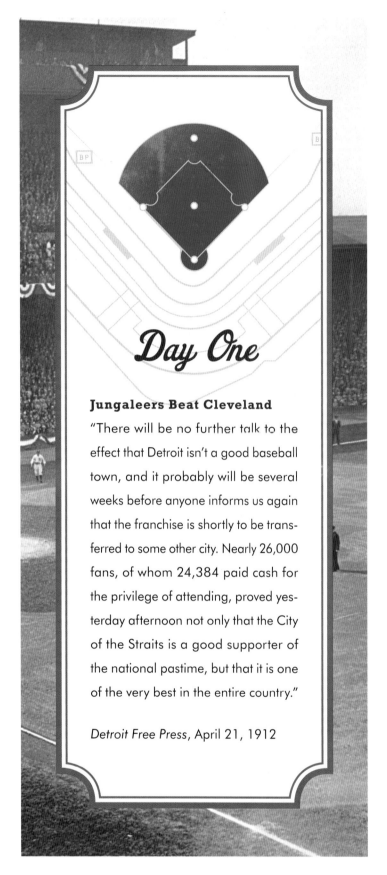

Day One

Jungaleers Beat Cleveland

"There will be no further talk to the effect that Detroit isn't a good baseball town, and it probably will be several weeks before anyone informs us again that the franchise is shortly to be transferred to some other city. Nearly 26,000 fans, of whom 24,384 paid cash for the privilege of attending, proved yesterday afternoon not only that the City of the Straits is a good supporter of the national pastime, but that it is one of the very best in the entire country."

Detroit Free Press, April 21, 1912

While Fenway has been rehabbed and Wrigley even got lights after 76 years, Tiger Stadium met the same fate as Ebbets Field and the Polo Grounds, falling to the wrecking balls in 2008 after seeing its final game played in 1999. As we'll see, a big civic rising was not enough to save the ol' yard.

Tiger Stadium was not pretty. It was not a jewel of a bandbox or friendly in its confines or majestic in its sweeping arcs. It was, after its various additions over the years, basically a cube without a top. It had poles standing in front of numerous seats. It had a boring paint scheme. It had few luxuries, exposed piping, roll-up doors, and only a handful of late-arriving amenities. It was, as so many people have commented, a reflection of the blue-collar nature of the city itself.

It's easy from afar to love a wacky green wall or decorative ivy-covered bricks. It's easy to thrill at World Series after World Series in a House That Ruth Built. You don't have to be a Dodgers fan, young or old, to "remember when" and dream up visions of Ebbets.

But Tiger Stadium? That's for locals only. Detroiters know how much the yard meant to the team and to the city. Sadly, it was only the new owners of the team and the city officials who, in the end, didn't recognize that. The flags still wave on the flagpole that stood in center field for 100 years, but that pole stands now above what is basically an empty lot.

However, on that lot dance glorious ghosts. Who needs a cornfield to have a field of dreams?

THE CORNER

The corner of Michigan and Trumbull in the pre-auto 1890s was the site of a haymarket—the early version of a giant gas station, one might say. The owner of the Western League's Detroit franchise bought the site and built a ballpark there. It wasn't much, just an L-shaped set of bleachers. The dirt put down to form the infield was placed directly atop the cobblestones that formed the market's floor, making for an occasionally

— ★ —

ABOVE: Nothing to see on an off-day at Tiger Stadium, but if you ended up with a seat behind one of the iron beams shown here, you'd have trouble seeing anything anyway. "Obstructed-view" seats were sold for a discount, however.

ENCLOSED 1: Catcher Jason Varitek is featured on this Monster seat ticket from 2003, the first season in which fans could climb to that lofty perch to watch a game.

ENCLOSED 2: The 1934 World Series featured nine future Hall of Fame performers . . . and one Hall of Shame performance by Detroit fans. This is the game program cover from that series.

CHARLES W. BENNETT, THE RELIABLE AND PLUCKY CATCHER.

TOP: The concept of covering a ballpark with advertising is not new, of course, and Bennett Field's walls offered appeals to fans from a wide variety of merchants.

ABOVE: Longevity, loyalty, and a bit of tragedy combined to give former Detroit catcher Charlie Bennett the honor of having the ballpark named for him.

bumpy surface. The ballpark took on the name of Bennett Field after former team catcher Charlie Bennett. After a long career with the N.L.'s Detroit Wolverines and Boston Beaneaters, Bennett lost his legs after slipping under a train in 1894. But he was beloved by the hometown folks and not only was the ballpark first named for him, he caught or threw the ceremonial first pitch of each season from 1896 until his death in early 1927.

When the Tigers joined the new American League for the 1900 season, Bennett Field joined the big leagues. And what a debut! Heading into the bottom of the ninth against Milwaukee on opening day, the Tigers trailed 13–4. But a series of clutch hits (including four ground-rule doubles) led to an explosion of runs and the Tigers came back to win 14–13. Even now, 112 years later, no team has matched that last-inning comeback.

After Bennett Field first arrived at Michigan and Trumbull in 1896, it cemented the location as Detroit's baseball hub in the 20th century. This is the more modern Tiger Stadium.

Over the next decade, Michigan and Trumbull was witness to some pretty great baseball, though, until 1907, never on Sundays. Like many major cities, Detroit had "blue laws" that forbid such extravagance as a baseball game on the day of rest. To get around this, for a couple of seasons (1901–1902), then-owner James Burns erected a temporary field on his large property in the suburbs, to the west of the city lines. By 1907, the laws had been relaxed. While baseball on the Sabbath returned to downtown Detroit, Burns Park returned to pastureland.

HERE COMES COBB

In 1906 a fiery youngster from Georgia moved into a permanent place in the Detroit outfield. Over the next 22 seasons, he would gain a place among baseball immortals. As it was, in those early years, he led the Tigers to three straight A.L. pennants (1907–1909), becoming a hero throughout his adopted home state. He was not exactly fan friendly, angering teammates and hometown rooters almost as much as he infuriated opponents with his win-at-all-costs (and then some) attitude. He was selfish, rude, probably racist, ornery, and mean . . . but give this to Tyrus Raymond "Ty" Cobb—the man could play the game.

Cobb earned the first of his record 12 A.L. batting titles in 1907, his first full season in the majors. He also led the league in steals six times, the first in '07. (That was also the year that former team bookkeeper Frank Navin invested $40,000 in the team; he would have a big influence on the Corner in the ensuing years.) By the time he was finished, he had more hits, runs, steals, and batting titles than any player, and though some of his marks have since been topped, Cobb remains one of baseball's immortals.

For Tigers fans, he was a favorite from the start and his success made the Corner one of the centerpieces of the young American League. Though they lost three straight World Series, the Tigers' solid play helped to legitimize the new major league.

The team's success energized Detroit, a city then growing quickly as the auto industry picked up (or, should we say, pushed aside) steam. So popular were the Tigers over the years that enterprising neighbors had taken advantage of the low height of the outfield bleachers at Bennett Field to erect wildcat bleachers. Similar to what some folks have done on buildings bordering Wrigley Field, landlords along National Avenue behind left field in Detroit stacked up wooden seats on their roofs and charged folks to watch the game from afar. The practice was around from the earliest days of the park—since those seats were cheaper, they always sold—but the practice really cranked up for the big World Series games. A solution, from the team's point of view, was to build taller but temporary bleachers inside the park for use during the 1909 World Series. The idea was such a hit that the bleachers were made permanent for 1910, thus blocking the wildcatters.

Oh, sure, Ty Cobb is smiling here, but that's not the look that opponents saw when they faced the fiery—but enormously talented—Tigers outfielder.

But Bennett Field was starting to bulge at the seams. As fans packed the old place for a glimpse of the Georgia Peach and his mates, it became clear that if the team made room for more, then more could come . . . and pay. So was Tiger Stadium the House That Cobb Built? You could say that. It was in many ways thanks to the Tigers' run of success at the end of the first decade of the 20th century that the team gained enough popularity (i.e., income) to make a bigger ballpark worthwhile.

THE MODERN AGE

After the end of the 1911 season, Navin invested $300,000 to build a new concrete-and-steel ballpark, replacing Bennett Field. Osborn Engineering Company of Cleveland designed a concrete-and-steel structure that

Top 10 Moments at
TIGER STADIUM

★ ★ ★

(in chronological order)

April 20, 1912

Opening day. Ty Cobb's steal of home highlights a win by the home team in their new park.

April 30, 1922

Though it was a big game for the opponent, Detroit was the site and the Tigers were the victim of an amazing perfect game pitched by Chicago's Charlie Robertson.

October 9, 1934

Not Detroit's finest hour, but a memorable moment in World Series history, as Tigers fans lob garbage at St. Louis outfielder Joe Medwick late in an 11–0 blowout that gave the Cardinals the title.

October 7, 1935

Walk-off World Series! The Tigers earn their first world championship at Michigan and Trumbull, knocking off the Cubs at home.

May 2, 1939

The Yankees' star Lou Gehrig doesn't play in a game . . . for the first time in 2,130 games.

July 8, 1941

Boston's Ted Williams clubs a three-run homer to win the All-Star Game for the A.L. His jig as he headed to first after hitting it is a classic clip.

October 14, 1984

Another World Series title lands in Detroit, thanks in large part to slugger Kirk Gibson's two homers.

October 2–4, 1987

Capping a great late-season comeback, the Tigers sweep a series from the Blue Jays to earn the A.L. East division title.

August 25, 1990

Detroit's Cecil Fielder becomes one of only a handful of players to hit a homer over the left field roof.

September 27, 1999

The final game is played at Tiger Stadium.

Bennett Field and the Tigers played host to this World Series game in 1909. Though the Tigers reveled in three straight A.L. titles, they didn't enjoy losing three straight series.

seated 23,000, almost double the capacity of Bennett Field. The project would have cost about $50 million by today's standards. For his investment and energy, the owner/builder renamed his new gem Navin Field.

During the construction, home plate was moved from its original spot on the actual northeast corner of Michigan and Trumbull. It rotated up a block so that home plate was actually now at Michigan and National, while Michigan and Trumbull became the right field corner. This kept left-handed batters from having to look into the sun as often (and please note that Ty Cobb was a lefty). Navin also had a large canvas sheet placed in center field where seats would normally have been. Instead of watching the ball come out of the pitcher's hand from amid a pack of fans, batters now had a clear view of the ball. The "batter's backdrop" became standard in ballparks in just a few years.

It would not be called Tiger Stadium until 1961, but on April 20, 1912, the ballpark that would define the Tigers was opened to the public. The new palace held about 23,000 folks in a single deck of covered seats along with an open bleachers section in right field at Cherry and Trumbull. Charlie Bennett continued a tradition and caught the ceremonial first pitch, and, fittingly, Cobb had a big hand in the team's opening day win, stealing home in the first inning of a 6–5 win over Cleveland.

The new ballpark was a hit and the Tigers' attendance climbed steadily as the city grew with more and more automotive plants. The team led the A.L. in attendance in 1919 and in 1924 became the second team, after the Yankees, to draw one million fans. That total was aided by the addition of left field bleachers after the 1923 season. The team convinced the city to close up what

NAVIN PARK, DETROIT, MICH.

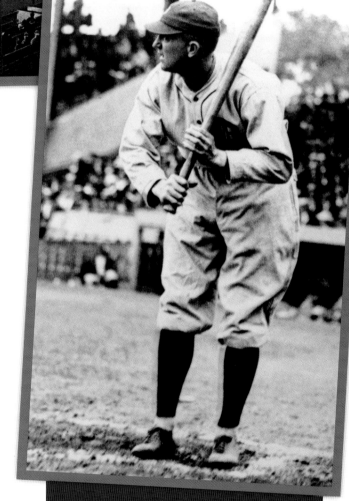

had been Cherry Street to let the ballpark expand outward enough to allow the new seats. A second deck spanning the area between first to third bases was also added at that time.

On the field, the team was not quite as good as the fans hoped, finishing third or lower every year from 1917 to 1934 (with the exception of a second-place finish in 1923). Cobb had taken over as player-manager in 1921 but could not rally his players to reach his own high levels of excellence. The Tigers posted winning records in all but one of his seasons at the helm, but other clubs were always better.

Of particular note in that era was a game in 1922. Cobb was still at the height of his powers and Detroit had one of the best-hitting teams in the league. However, at Navin Field on April 30, a White Sox rookie named Charlie Robertson threw a perfect game against the Tigers. It was the first perfect game in baseball since Cy Young's back in 1904, and though others have been thrown since,

TOP: This hand-colored postcard of Navin Field shows the deep single decks, the overhanging roof, and the separate right field bleacher section.

ABOVE: Cobb used this unique batting style to amass 4,189 hits, second-most all-time, and the top career batting average ever at .366.

Imagine Buster Posey of today's Giants not only winning the MVP award but also managing his new team to the World Series . . . and you get an idea of Mickey Cochrane's impressive 1934 campaign in Detroit.

More Than Just
THE TIGERS

★ ★ ★

Baseball:

Detroit Stars (Negro National League), 1920–1937; Detroit Danger women's baseball team, 2001

Football:

Detroit Lions (NFL), 1938–1975 (except 1940)

Soccer:

Detroit Cougars, 1967

Robertson's remains perhaps the most unlikely. Cobb claimed that the rookie was throwing a spitball or a shineball, offering numerous marked balls to the umpires as evidence. As evidence perhaps of umpires' disinterest in assisting the combative Cobb, his pleas were ignored.

CHAMPIONS AT LAST

After the 1926 season, an era ended in Detroit when Cobb left. He played two more short seasons with the Philadelphia Athletics before hanging up two of the busiest and most successful spikes in the game. His legacy in Detroit could be seen every time Navin Field was filled for a big game.

The next big star to arrive in Detroit brought with him a career that was already at Hall of Fame levels.

Catcher Mickey Cochrane had already won an MVP award and three World Series with the Athletics when he joined Detroit in 1934 as player-manager. He led the Tigers back to the A.L. pennant, while batting .320 and winning another MVP trophy. "Black Mike" was a godsend to Detroit. Under his leadership on and off the field, the Tigers returned to the top of the American League.

In the 1934 World Series, they faced the mighty "Gashouse Gang" of the St. Louis Cardinals. The Tigers took the series to seven games, with the finale played at Navin Field. However, the Cardinals took pitcher Elden Auker to the woodshed, scoring seven runs in the third inning. After Cardinals outfielder Joe "Ducky" Medwick made a hard slide late in the game, Tigers fans responded by throwing garbage when Medwick

Red-white-and-blue bunting signals that this is more than just a game at Navin Field. In fact, it's action from the 1934 World Series. Also note the CBS sign high on the third deck; national radio broadcasts of the series had been around for more than a decade by this time.

took his spot on the field for the final inning. After doing some ducking, Ducky had to be escorted from the field before order was restored. Then the fans had to watch the ignominy of an opposing team celebrating on the "enemy" diamond.

The celebration went the other way in 1935, however. Again led by Cochrane and by stars Charlie Gehringer, Goose Goslin, and Hank Greenberg (more about him in a moment), the Tigers were the class of the A.L. again. In the World Series, they faced the Chicago

Cubs. The Tigers needed one more win in game 6 to clinch the series, but they needed a bit of drama to bring the hometown fans the long-awaited championship. With the game tied 3–3 in the bottom of the ninth, Cochrane singled and moved to second on a sacrifice. Goslin rapped a single to right field that allowed the 32-year-old skipper/catcher to skip home with the series-winning run. Finally, the Corner had a champion.

SOME GLORIOUS SEASONS

Frank Navin didn't live to see the team try to defend their title, however. The man who had built Navin Field and brought in the stars that brought home a title died just a month after the World Series concluded.

New owner Walter Briggs, perhaps inspired both by Navin's building success and the team's solid play,

pumped a million bucks into Navin Field. Briggs had his builders carry the double-decking all the way around the park. All but the deepest center field bleachers were covered, too. The newly renamed Briggs Stadium (hey, when you pay for it, you can name it) became one of sport's biggest venues as capacity reached a capacious 53,000.

In order to get the double-decking to work in the tight confines of the right field corner, the upper deck was extended to 10 feet over the playing field itself. That is, a high fly ball that might have landed in a fielder's glove on the warning track could now be interrupted on

Famous Firsts

These link to the 1912 rebirth of the "new" Navin Field, rather than the 1896 birth of Bennett Field on the same site.

First Win: April 20, 1912, Tigers defeat Cleveland 6–5

First Hit: Unknown

First Home Run: Del Pratt, St. Louis Browns, May 5, 1912

First Championship: 1935, Tigers over Cardinals

. . . and Lasts

Last Game: September 27, 1999, Tigers defeat Royals 9–2

Last Hit: Robert Fick, Tigers, September 27, 1999

Last Home Run: Robert Fick, September 27, 1999

Last Championship: 1984, Tigers over Padres

its descent by a few rows of seats—the world's cheapest home runs.

The expanded seating also made it attractive for another sport: football. In 1938, the NFL's Detroit Lions found a perfect place to play at Briggs. With the exception of one year, the Lions would make their home there until 1975, when they, like so many businesses and people from Detroit, left the city for the suburbs. In 1953 and 1956, the Lions won the NFL Championship Game at the field. Their 59–14 pasting of the Browns in 1959 was the last time that a Detroit team ended a season atop the NFL . . . and it happened at the Corner.

Three years after the expansion, on May 2, 1939, another opponent made history at Briggs Stadium, though it was an occasion that would turn out not to be one to celebrate. Yankees great Lou Gehrig had played 2,130 consecutive games when he arrived at Briggs that morning. Feeling poorly and not playing anywhere near his immortal standards, he told manager Joe McCarthy to keep him out of the lineup. The then-longest playing streak in the game ended with Gehrig sitting on the dugout steps in Detroit.

The next year, the Tigers won the A.L. for the third time in seven years, but fell in the World Series to the Reds. Bobo Newsom pitched valiantly for Detroit, winning a pair of games. But he couldn't hold on in the finale, giving up two runs in the seventh. Meanwhile, Cincy's Paul Derringer allowed only one unearned run and the Tigers went home to Detroit in second place again.

In 1941, another legend left baseball, though only temporarily. This time around it was Tigers superstar Hank Greenberg. Greenberg was the 1935 MVP when he led the league in homers and RBI. He approached Ruth's single-season record with 58 dingers in 1938 and in 1940 led the A.L. again with 41 homers and 150 RBI.

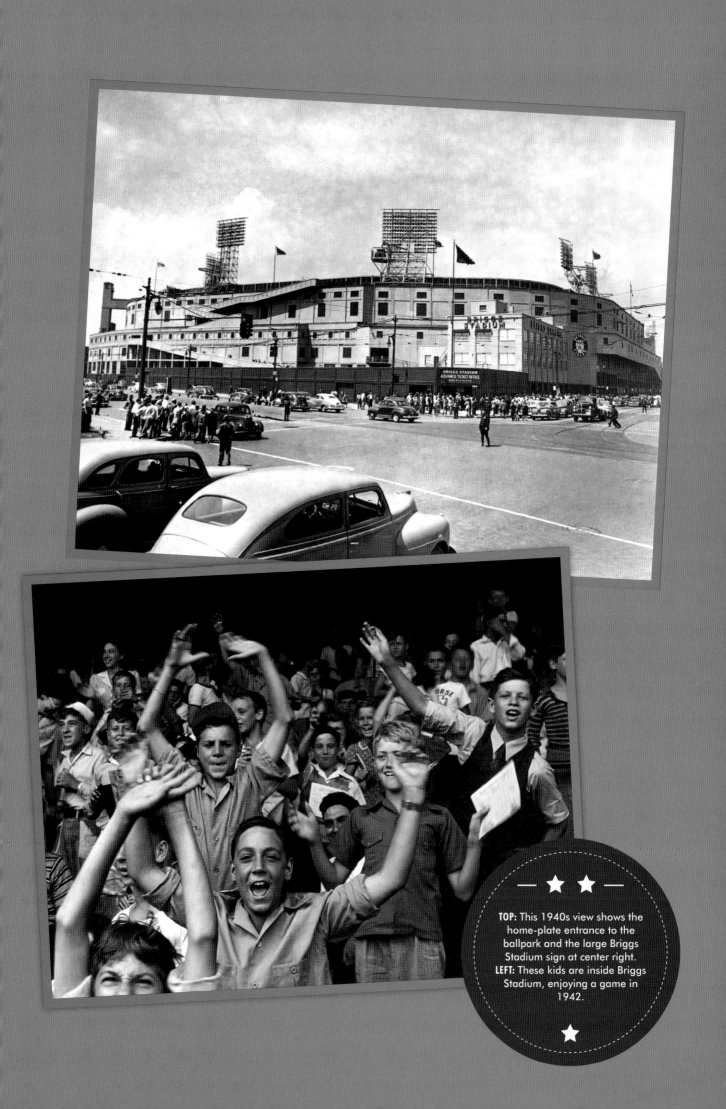

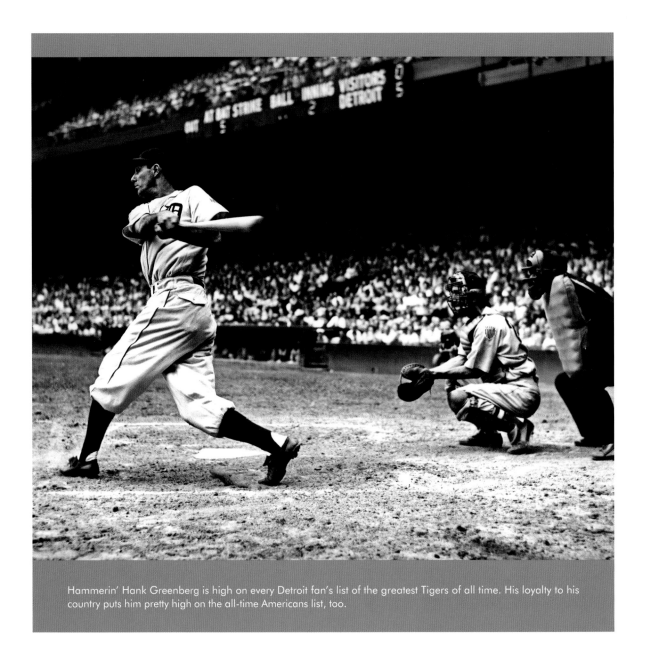

Hammerin' Hank Greenberg is high on every Detroit fan's list of the greatest Tigers of all time. His loyalty to his country puts him pretty high on the all-time Americans list, too.

But with World War II looming, Greenberg was drafted into the Army. He served from May until December 5, 1941. Draft rules were changed at that point, releasing anyone over 30 from serving.

The rules changed two days later when the Japanese bombed Pearl Harbor. Greenberg, who could have stayed out of the service, reenlisted almost immediately and spent the next few years at war while the Tigers battled on without him back home. Greenberg gave up almost four full seasons in the prime of his career, giving fans around the country a much deeper reason for honoring the big slugger.

While he was away, Briggs Stadium was the site of one of the most memorable All-Star Games ever. Held on July 8, 1941, the game, which had started only back in 1933, featured all-time heroes such as Joe DiMaggio, Mel Ott, Carl Hubbell, Bill Dickey, Jimmie Foxx, and Red Ruffing. But it was a slim young swinger from Boston who came home the hero. With two outs in the bottom of the ninth, Ted Williams slammed a pitch from Claude Passeau well into the right field seats for a three-run, walk-off homer. Though Williams would become known for showing an often-sour disposition on the field, seeing the then-young man dancing a happy jig as he rounded the bases after his big blast is a wonderful lasting memory of the player, the moment, and the setting.

Greenberg came back in 1945 in time to help the Tigers wrap up the A.L. pennant. They faced the Cubs again but this time came out on top, winning another World Series title (though the final game was played at Wrigley Field). Greenberg had two homers and seven RBI while batting .304 in the series, a fitting capper to his years of heroism. In both 1944 and 1945, the Tigers also boasted the league's best pitcher, "Prince" Hal Newhouser. The Prince won the MVP award both seasons, the first pitcher to earn the honor in back-to-back years.

In 1968, known as the Year of the Pitcher, Tigers starter Denny McLain had himself a career year. He went 31–6 and also led the A.L. with 28 complete games, earning both the MVP and Cy Young Awards.

THE TIGERS ROAR AGAIN

The next big story at Briggs Stadium happened at night—or on lots of nights. In 1948, lights were added to the ballpark. Detroit was the last place in the A.L. where fans could watch only in the day (the Cubs, of course, were the last in the bigs to brighten the night, installing lights in 1988). Remember that tricky right field overhang? It was big enough that it put the right field wall in shadow at night games, so lights were put under the overhang to make sure fielders could see the wall, if not the ball.

Though the Corner had been home to baseball since 1896, in 1961 it finally became home to Tiger Stadium. The ballpark got its new name and the team put together a second-place finish, its best year in a decade. Slugging first baseman Norm Cash was a key player; he hit 41 dingers in '61.

The next big year for the Tigers came in 1968, when they used an amazing one-two pitching punch to win the A.L. by 12 games. Right-hander Denny McLain won 31 games, the last pitcher in the majors to top 30, while lefty Mickey Lolich won 17, as well as a trio of games in the World Series against the Cardinals.

Anchoring the offense for Detroit was outfielder Al Kaline, one of the greatest Tigers ever. A regular from

1968 WORLD SERIES

TIGER STADIUM • DETROIT

OFFICIAL SOUVENIR

★ ★

To get Tigers hero Al Kaline in the 1968 World Series lineup (he had missed a lot of time with a broken arm earlier), the Tigers moved outfielder Mickey Stanley to short. It was a good move: Kaline hit .379 in the series and the Tigers won in seven games.

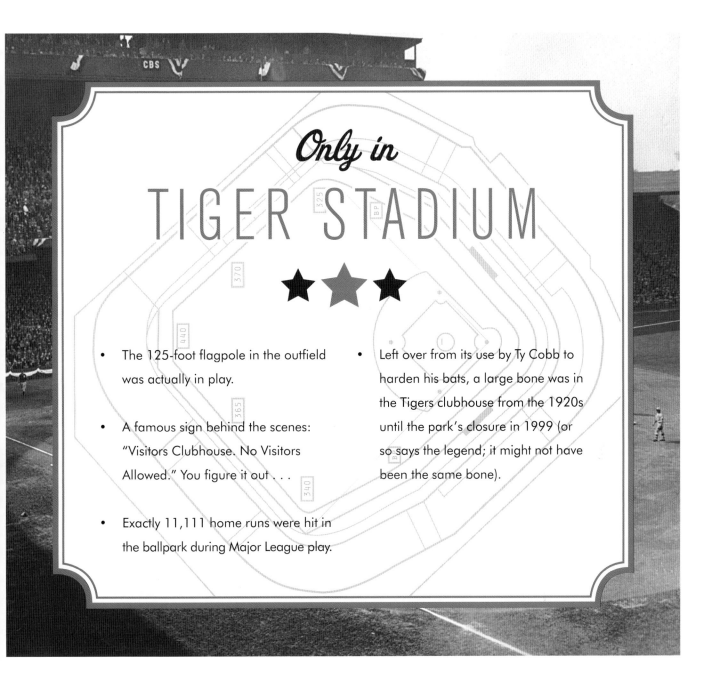

Only in
TIGER STADIUM

★ ★ ★

- The 125-foot flagpole in the outfield was actually in play.

- A famous sign behind the scenes: "Visitors Clubhouse. No Visitors Allowed." You figure it out . . .

- Exactly 11,111 home runs were hit in the ballpark during Major League play.

- Left over from its use by Ty Cobb to harden his bats, a large bone was in the Tigers clubhouse from the 1920s until the park's closure in 1999 (or so says the legend; it might not have been the same bone).

1954 to 1974, Kaline was a .297 career hitter who also won 10 Gold Gloves, among the most ever. His gentlemanly, humble attitude endeared him to a generation of Tigers fans, all of whom wished he could have notched one more homer—he ended his career with 399.

It's also noteworthy that attendance for the 1968 season topped two million for the first time.

In 1971, another All-Star Game was held at Michigan and Trumbull. The fully enclosed ballpark made for tempting targets for sluggers hoping to clear the outfield roofs. Only a handful accomplished the feat, and only four—Harmon Killebrew in 1962, Frank Howard in 1968, Cecil Fielder in 1990, and Mark McGwire in 1997—did so in left. One of the most famous attempts came in that '71 Midsummer Classic. Reggie Jackson was a young slugger several years away from his Mr. October feats. Against the N.L.'s Dock Ellis, Jackson slammed a moon shot that soared so majestically toward the rooftop that he paused, bat in hand, at home plate to watch. It cleared the roof with ease but struck a light standard. It's still regarded as one of the "biggest" home runs at Tiger Stadium, though it didn't make it into the actual neighborhood.

Tiger Stadium was the nest for one of the most unique personalities in baseball history when Mark "the Bird" Fidrych landed in 1976.

THE BIRD LANDS AND GIBSON GOES YARD

A rare period of excitement came in 1976 when the Bird landed in Detroit. Mark Fidrych, a 21-year-old right-hander, burst onto the baseball scene by leading the A.L. with a 2.34 ERA and a remarkable 24 complete games. He won 19 of them, but it was how he acted that got the most attention. A tall, gawky dude, he talked to baseballs. He galumphed around the diamond. He hugged teammates. He was, in other words, almost as unbaseball-y a player as you could imagine. His talents and his quirks made him national news. Sadly, injuries grounded the Bird, who pitched briefly in four more seasons before flying off to roost.

Another important moment in Tiger Stadium's history came rather quietly in 1978 when the Tigers sold the stadium to the city for $1 and a favorable long-term lease. Then, in 1983, the team was sold to pizza magnate Tom Monaghan, who said he would keep Tiger Stadium standing. Good timing on the sale. The 1984 Tigers team was one of the most dominant big-league clubs. They set a record by winning 35 of their first 40 games and never looked back. The middle infield was anchored by shortstop Alan Trammell and second baseman Lou Whitaker, who played together in Detroit for 19 seasons (1977–1995). Slugging outfielder Kirk Gibson brought his football-player mentality to the field, while starting pitching star Jack Morris reminded fans of their own blue-collar work mentality. In the bullpen, Willie Hernandez was so dominant as a closer that he was named the Cy Young Award winner and the A.L. MVP, a rare combination.

Detroit finished 15 games up on the Yankees, clinching the pennant by early September. They brushed aside the Royals in the ALCS in three games. In the World Series, they faced the San Diego Padres and the two teams split the first pair of games in San Diego.

The Tigers made sure they didn't have to head west again.

In game 3, a four-spot in the second led to an easy 5–2 win. In game 4, a homer by Trammell helped Morris win, 4–2. And then came game 5.

On a Sunday evening, October 14, 1984, the old ballyard at Michigan and Trumbull saw perhaps its highlight moment. There had been some pretty darned good players who had run in its grass, and they'd accomplished some impressive things. But for sheer drama, for perfect timing, for spotlight success, none of them matched Kirk Gibson in game 5.

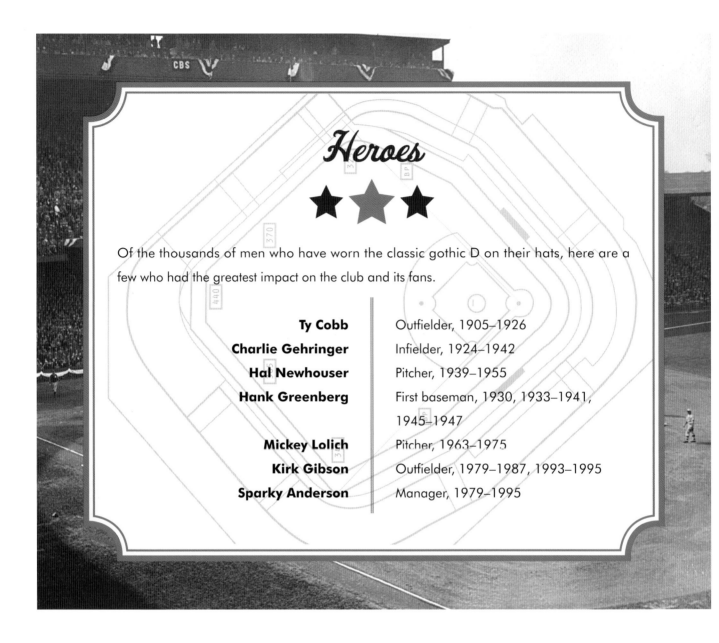

Heroes

★ ★ ★

Of the thousands of men who have worn the classic gothic D on their hats, here are a few who had the greatest impact on the club and its fans.

Ty Cobb	Outfielder, 1905–1926
Charlie Gehringer	Infielder, 1924–1942
Hal Newhouser	Pitcher, 1939–1955
Hank Greenberg	First baseman, 1930, 1933–1941, 1945–1947
Mickey Lolich	Pitcher, 1963–1975
Kirk Gibson	Outfielder, 1979–1987, 1993–1995
Sparky Anderson	Manager, 1979–1995

In the bottom of the first, Gibson smacked a two-run homer to deep center field. In the fifth, with the score tied 3–3, he scored from third on a sac fly. Padres catcher Terry Kennedy had no chance against the former Michigan State All-American wide receiver. Finally, in the bottom of the eighth, clinging to a one-run lead, the Tigers had two men on. Up stepped Gibson, who powered a long homer into the left field seats to cinch the game and clinch the series. (Gibson, of course, would later top himself with a dramatic game-winning homer in game 1 of the 1988 World Series for the Dodgers.)

Sadly, Detroit fans hoping for a long life for their beloved ballpark shot themselves in the foot after the victory. Scenes of the car-burning, store-looting "celebration" in the streets of Detroit gave more fuel to the drive to get rid of the Corner Dinosaur.

BEGINNING OF THE END

Three years later, the Tigers did give their fans and the ballpark one last trip to the postseason, and they did it in dramatic fashion. Entering the final home series of the year, they trailed the visiting Blue Jays by a game. Detroit swept the series and captured the A.L. East crown by two games. The capper was a gutsy 1–0 shutout thrown by Frank Tanana. Detroit lost to Minnesota in the ALCS, however.

That series was, in many ways, a last hurrah for the ballpark. The Tigers finished a game back of Boston

A smattering of fans spread across the center field bleachers in the background of this shot from behind home plate.

the next year, but didn't sniff the playoffs again before the ballpark's final season in 1999.

The end of Tiger Stadium was actually rather long and drawn-out, as numerous civic and governmental groups explored a variety of ways to save the ballpark. They even organized a "group hug" around the entire exterior of Tiger Stadium in 1988 to symbolize the community's love. The ballpark was placed on the National Register of Historic Places, but even that wouldn't save it.

Various attempts at a renovation plan were put forth (fan polls, not surprisingly, showed renovation favored over a new ballpark by about three to one). A privately funded scheme called the Cochrane Plan, in honor of the team's long-ago player-manager, was put forth in 1990, but the owners of the ball club and the ballpark paid little attention. The plan created extensions and additions to the existing yard, adding more amenities and even some luxury boxes. But the costs were extensive and the lure of a spanking-new, luxury-box-swaddled

Sure, it's nice, but it's not the same. Comerica Park opened for the 2000 season, leaving Michigan and Trumbull to the dustbin of baseball history.

park remained out there (especially after the successful openings of new parks with old-time themes in Baltimore and Cleveland).

A second pizza magnate, Mike Ilitch, took over the team in 1992. (Monaghan was Domino's, Ilitch Little Caesar's.) But by then the writing was on the wall, although acres of trees and gallons of ink were used to write in support of keeping a renovated ballpark. Tiger Stadium was heading toward its end. It became official as ground broke on the new Comerica Park in 1997 that the end was in sight for Navin Field, Briggs Stadium, and Tiger Stadium.

The final game was played on September 27, 1999. It was surrounded by ceremonies, and after the final out in

a Tigers' win, home plate was removed and transported to the new site. A commemorative flag was lowered for the last time and passed, hand to hand, through a long series of Tigers greats. Kaline, Gibson, Trammell, and Whitaker were among them, of course, as well as the Bird. Relatives of Bennett, Briggs, and Navin were also in attendance to help close the circle.

As Ernie Harwell, the team's longtime, beloved Hall of Fame announcer, slowly read a final prose poem to Tiger Stadium, the banks of lights went out one by one. And it was over.

As preservationists fought on into the 21st century against the city, Tiger Stadium, shuttered and fenced off, lingered as a painful white-elephant reminder of a

Detroit that used to be, of a ballpark that used to ring with the cheers of thousands. It was finally demolished, save for a few walls and the sturdy flagpole, in 2009.

In April 2012, Tiger Stadium would have been 100 years old. While Fenway Park, its baseball twin, enjoyed a slew of honors, events, publications, and parties, Tiger lived on only in memories. The ball field that still exists at Michigan and Trumbull hosted a small and muted celebration. The flagpole that still stands where once Ty Cobb roamed flew a special centennial banner.

The banner was made and strung up by a group who have made it their life's mission to make sure that Tiger Stadium remains in the hearts of Detroit fans. Peter Riley, one of the key members of the group, along with Charlie Greiner and Tom Derry, was pretty peeved that the hometown team did nothing to mark the centennial.

Riley said at the time, "It's a crime, but it's the reality of the matter. Even to me, somebody who has been watching this play out for a long time, I can't say I'm the least surprised. It's a shame and hurtful to those who still remain and everyone who remembers what used to be."

Detroit fans now enjoy Comerica Park, one of the slew of new parks added in the first part of the 21st century. But there remain a diehard few who loved the old, plain, sturdy Tiger Stadium. If you're ever in Detroit, make sure and head to Michigan and Trumbull and say hello to the ghosts.

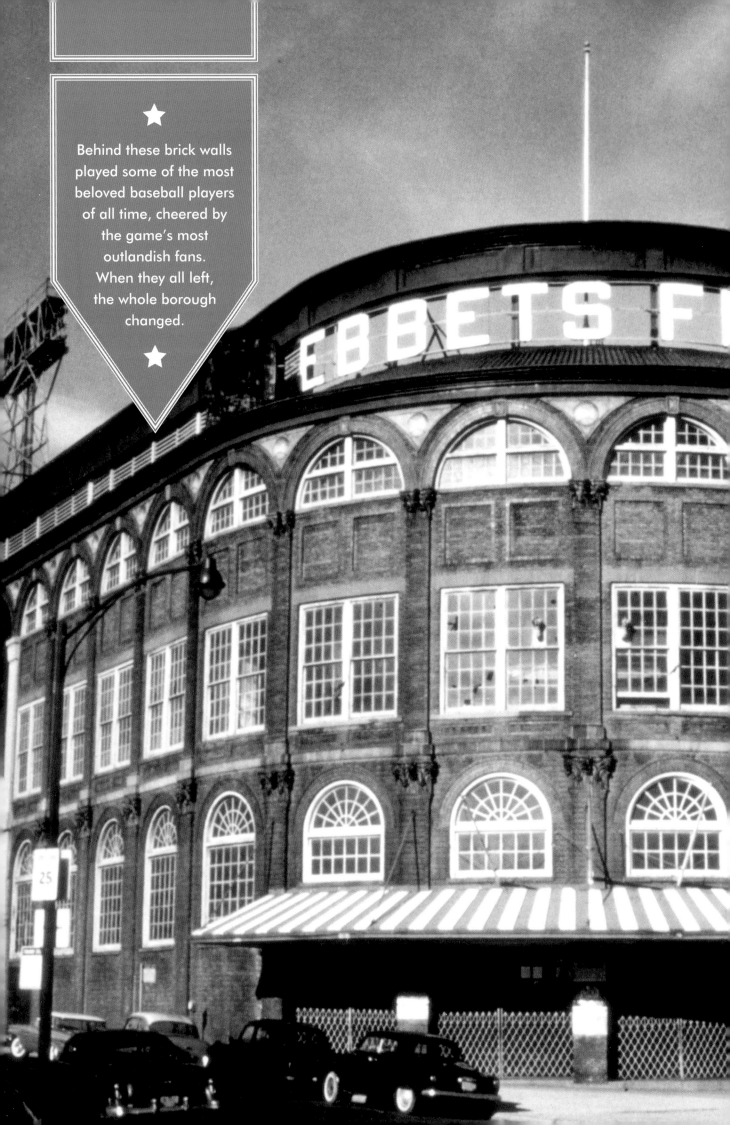

Behind these brick walls played some of the most beloved baseball players of all time, cheered by the game's most outlandish fans. When they all left, the whole borough changed.

CHAPTER FIVE

EBBETS FIELD

BROOKLYN, N.Y.

YEAR BUILT	1912–1913
HOME TEAM	Brooklyn Dodgers
FIRST GAME	April 9, 1913
LAST GAME	September 24, 1957
CAPACITY (AVERAGE)	33,000
FAMOUS FEATURES	Outfield signs, famous fans, oft-tragic team

It was built on a garbage dump. Its teams won only one championship in its 44-year run in the majors. It was not pretty by any stretch of the imagination. But even more than 50 years after it was smashed to pieces (by the same wrecking ball that would only two years later destroy the Polo Grounds), Ebbets Field remains in the eyes of baseball history a magical and shiny place where wacky characters romped on and off the field, and where a specially connected set of fans and players found a nesting place for their undying love.

When the Dodgers left Brooklyn and Ebbets Field after the 1957 season, it was, to many locals, the end of

★ ★

Two ways to see a game at Ebbets Field: The top photo, probably staged, shows Commissioner Kenesaw M. Landis joining kids for a "knot-hole gang" view of the game; the bottom photo offers a rarely seen view of the Ebbets Field grand-stands from the outside.

★

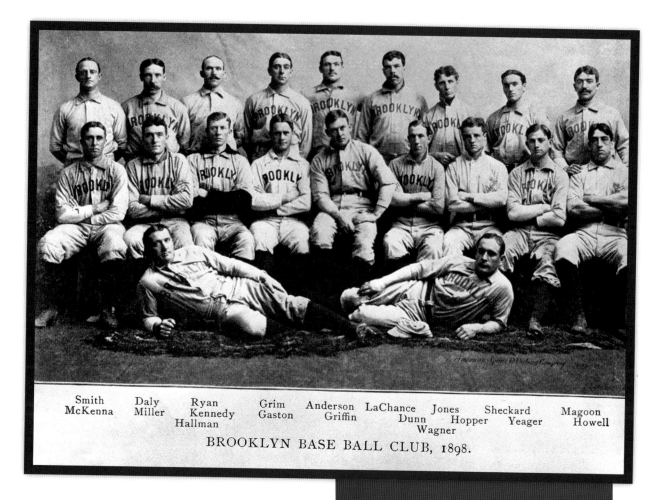

Smith
McKenna
Daly
Miller
Ryan
Kennedy
Hallman
Grim
Gaston
Anderson
Griffin
LaChance
Jones
Dunn
Wagner
Hopper
Sheckard
Yeager
Magoon
Howell

BROOKLYN BASE BALL CLUB, 1898.

Life before Ebbets: Brooklyn had a team in the National League from 1890. Here in 1898 they were the Bridegrooms.

an era. New York City had gobbled up Brooklyn in 1898, but the borough long retained its aura of otherness, its unique character that set it apart from the rest of the metropolis. The Dodgers were the living embodiment of that otherness and Ebbets Field was the place in which it was all celebrated. The story of Ebbets Field is certainly one of steel and concrete and walls, but it was, more than most ballparks, the story of the people in the seats. The team certainly made its mark, but it was the fans who packed Ebbets Field that make it so memorable.

And, of course, for one moment in 1947, it was the most important place in America.

DODGING THE TROLLEYS

A Brooklyn team had been part of the National League since 1890, having moved from the American Association in which they began in 1884. The club was known by numerous names, including the Grays, Bridegrooms, Grooms, and Superbas. They had earned the nickname "Trolley Dodgers" in the late 1800s thanks to the need for fans to skip among the tracks that led to and surrounded their home in Washington Park in south Brooklyn. By the time they moved to Ebbets Field in 1913, Dodgers was the accepted name (though beloved manager Wilbert Robinson led most to call the team the Robins from 1914 until 1931).

Whatever they were called, the team played its first N.L. games at Third Avenue and First Street in the Red Hook section of the borough, that was, as noted, then a separate city. (By the way, big props if you know

that this park was the site of the only big-league appearance of Archie "Moonlight" Graham, whose name was given to the fictional character at the center of the movie *Field of Dreams*.)

The team's bookkeeper, Charles Ebbets, had slowly risen up the team ranks. By 1898, he was team president, and in 1907 he bought out the remaining shareholders to become the team's owner. He and the other team management had packed Washington Park as full as it could be packed, but upon assuming control, Ebbets resolved to move up and out.

If you build it, they will come, even if it is built on a garbage dump. That's the philosophy that Ebbets used to find a home for the new ballpark. He chose an area of the borough called Pigtown for its numerous empty and garbage-strewn lots. A shrewd businessman, he announced this intention to no one, but instead took up the quiet task of buying what would turn out to be more than a thousand small lots and landholdings to stitch together to make his

TOP: Once they located the flag (no one had thought to bring one), the team—in their warm-up sweaters—took part in pregame flag-raising ceremonies on opening day in 1913.

ABOVE: Ambitious and energetic, Ebbets had a long-term plan for the ballpark and the team. He took years to assemble the plots of land on which he saw his dream come true.

dream come true. It took him four years to gather the necessary plots and cost him so much he had to sell off half of his biggest asset: the Dodgers franchise itself.

However, his move proved prescient. By the time the park opened in 1913, the area had become the locus for a pair of subway lines, nine trolley lines, and a couple of wide boulevards useful for the growing number of automobiles. (Cars were never a big deal for the Dodgers; at their height, some accounts put the number of parking spaces near the ballpark at less than 1,000.) So he built it, and they came.

Designed by architect Clarence Randall Van Buskirk, Ebbets Field did not have the ornamental character of some of the other parks built in this era, such as Comiskey Park or Shibe Park. It was a workaday park for a blue-collar crowd. So limited were amenities that no one noticed that there was not a press box until reporters arrived for opening day. A few rows were roped off to accommodate the scribes, but an actual "box" would not be installed for more than a decade.

Double decks of seats flowed from third base all the way around home plate toward the right field corner. In the early edition of the park, there were no outfield bleachers. Overall, more than 22,000 folks could fill the place, more than double what Ebbets could squeeze into old Washington Park.

What the rest of the park lacked in style was more than made up for by the entryway rotunda. At the corner of Sullivan and McKeever Places, fans walked across an 80-foot-wide floor of Italian marble, crafted to look like baseball stitching. High above their heads in the two-story cupola hung a chandelier made of baseball bats and baseballs. (The Mets' home in Citi Field, though in a different borough, borrows lovingly from the Ebbets rotunda, though Ebbets didn't have escalators.)

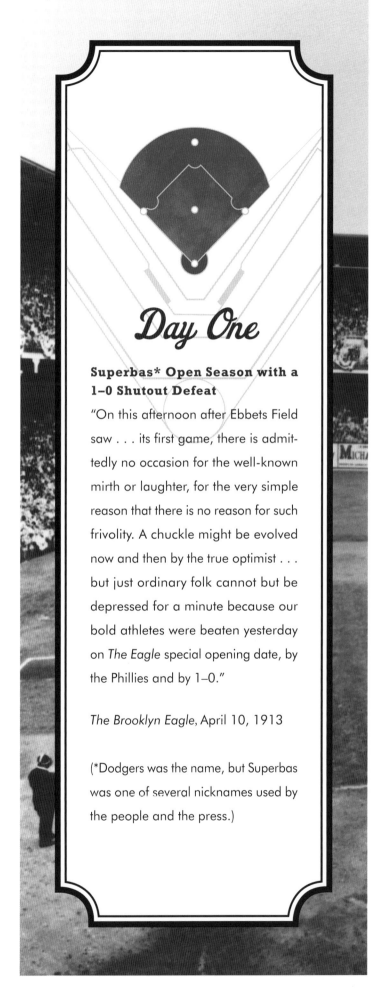

Day One

Superbas* Open Season with a 1–0 Shutout Defeat

"On this afternoon after Ebbets Field saw . . . its first game, there is admittedly no occasion for the well-known mirth or laughter, for the very simple reason that there is no reason for such frivolity. A chuckle might be evolved now and then by the true optimist . . . but just ordinary folk cannot but be depressed for a minute because our bold athletes were beaten yesterday on *The Eagle* special opening date, by the Phillies and by 1–0."

The Brooklyn Eagle, April 10, 1913

(*Dodgers was the name, but Superbas was one of several nicknames used by the people and the press.)

Here's a classic shot: A rare photo of action from the first game ever played at Ebbets Field, April 9, 1913.

On the other end of the quality spectrum, the metal fences in back of the outfield fences were made in such a way that kids could stand outside the park and peek in between cracks. Though these spying spots were not through wood, the freeloaders were said to be in the "knothole gang," a term that would be used for several kids' clubs founded by the team in ensuing years.

The ballpark itself had two small decks that started a bit past third base and curved right around to the right field foul pole. No outfield bleachers were in place on opening day. Conforming to nearby streets, right field was pretty close, only about 300 feet from home plate, while center field roamed out as far as 450 feet. In left field, it would take a good poke to clear the 419-foot distance. (Bleachers added to left field in 1926 made it a more reachable goal.)

In what might be seen as a symbol of the Dodgers' long-term lack of success, when Ebbets Field opened for business on April 9, 1913, along with the missing press box, it was realized on opening day that an American flag was nowhere to be found, nor were the keys to the front gate.

LET THE GAMES BEGIN

But open it did and away they went. On the field, the team was led by the type of colorful characters who would populate both field and seat for the next four decades. Casey Stengel, later the successful and beloved manager of the Yankees, was a Dodgers outfielder. His most famous stunt among many fan-pleasing moments was when he took his position in left field and tipped his hat, releasing a bird in salute to the fans. Zack

Dodgers outfielder Casey Stengel, later a Hall of Fame manager for the Yankees, shows off the latest in 1920s eyewear fashion, sporting shades while posing for a photo at Ebbets Field.

Top 10 Moments at
EBBETS FIELD

(in chronological order)

October 10, 1916

Brooklyn beats the Red Sox in the first World Series game at Ebbets Field. Of course, being the Dodgers, they lose the series in five games.

September 16, 1924

Bad news for Brooklyn as St. Louis Cardinals first baseman Jim Bottomley sets a single-game record by driving in 12 runs.

June 15, 1938

In the first night game in Ebbets Field, Johnny Vander Meer of the Reds makes history with his second consecutive no-hitter.

August 26, 1939

The first Major League game ever televised beams out from Ebbets Field to those tiny few people in New York City with televisions.

October 5, 1941

A dropped third strike by Dodgers catcher Mickey Owen gives the Yankees new life in the World Series and the Bombers come back to win it.

April 15, 1947

Playing first base for the Dodgers, Jackie Robinson becomes the first African American player in the majors in the 20th century.

October 3, 1947

Another opponent shines, as the Yankees' Bill Bevens comes within an out of the first World Series no-hitter. Brooklyn's Cookie Lavagetto spoils it.

July 12, 1949

In the only All-Star Game ever played at Ebbets, a trio of Dodgers—Robinson, Don Newcombe, and Roy Campanella, along with Larry Doby of the Indians—help break another line by becoming the first African Americans in the Midsummer Classic.

July 31, 1954

Boston Braves outfielder Joe Adcock has four homers and a double to set a record with 18 total bases.

October 3, 1955

The Dodgers win! The Dodgers win! The Dodgers win! Well, on this date, they record their third win of the World Series, on their way to capturing their one and only title while in Brooklyn.

The first three games of the seven-game, best-of-nine 1920 World Series were played at Ebbets Field. Before one of those games, fans patiently awaited the opening of the gates.

Wheat was the team's hitting star and one of the most unheralded of the pre–World War I heroes of baseball; he remains a century later among the team's all-time leaders in several offensive categories.

In 1916, as the Dodgers won the N.L. and played the Red Sox, Ebbets Field hosted its first World Series game. Boston had a great pitching staff, led by a young lefty named Babe Ruth and the hard-throwing Ernie Shore. Game 3 was at Ebbets, where the Dodgers had their only win of the series, 4–3. Boston ended up taking the series in five games.

Four years later, the World Series returned to Ebbets Field, but the Dodgers fell once again, this time in record-setting fashion. In game 5 in Cleveland, the Dodgers hit into the first and still the only unassisted triple play in World Series history. Indians shortstop Bill Wambsganss caught a line drive, stepped on second to double one runner, and tagged the runner from first, just like that. It didn't happen at Ebbets Field, but it was to become typical of the Dodgers' fortunes in the ensuing decades. Their 1920 pennant was the team's high-water mark until World War II.

TOP: To reach Bedford Road, the northeast boundary of the ballpark, fans could walk across center field to use a gate located in the upper left corner of this photo.

ABOVE: This later image shows the famous Schaefer beer sign (H for hit, E for error) and the massive Bulova clock, while down below Abe Stark dared hitters.

Ebbets, regardless of his team's consistent second-division finishes, was ready to expand. In 1931, he added a second deck, joining additional bleachers erected in 1926. Capacity reached its zenith at about 35,000. Also in 1931, the right field scoreboard was built, a structure that became Ebbets's visual calling card, much as Fenway has the Green Monster and Wrigley has the ivy.

Surrounded by revenue-generating advertising boards, the scoreboard wall had to be built in and around existing obstacles inside and outside the park. Extremely obsessive people once counted the number of angles and bends on the entire span of the outfield walls at 289. Playing in front of the wall was like being a flipper in a pinball machine.

Two of the ad signs became as well known as Fenway's Citgo. The first was for a local men's clothing store. Its largest letters spelled out ABE STARK, but next to the

More Than Just
THE DODGERS

★ ★ ★

Baseball:

Brooklyn Dodgers (N.L.), 1913–1957;

Brooklyn Eagles (Negro National League),

1935

Football:

Brooklyn Dodgers (NFL), 1930–1944;

Brooklyn Dodgers (AAFC), 1946–1948

name was a smaller sign that read HIT SIGN, WIN SUIT. Classic. Though only one player managed to sneak a ball past the right fielder and hit the wall there, 330 feet away (Woody English of the Dodgers in 1937), Stark's sign was certainly effective advertising. Stark himself became so well known that he ran for and was elected the president of the New York City Council and later president of the borough of Brooklyn.

The other famous scoreboard sign, though not erected until 1946, advertised Schaefer beer. Not only did the sign atop the right field scoreboard remind people of the "right beer to have when you're having more than one," as their memorable slogan went, but the sign itself took part in the game. When a player got a hit or error, the H or E in the name of the beer would light up to inform the patrons.

Also, above the scoreboard was a large round Bulova clock. In 1946, in a moment that would inspire a scene in *The Natural* decades later, Bama Rowell of the Braves

smacked a drive into the right field scoreboard that hit and smashed the large Bulova clock at the top of the wall. As Dodgers outfielder Dixie Walker dodged the flying glass, Rowell earned a double and a place in history.

Finally, according to Michael Gershman's *Diamonds*, one player was responsible for the addition of a 40-foot fence atop that right field wall. Babe Herman said it was to save the team money and keep neighbors happy: "I was breaking all the windows on the other side of Bedford Avenue" (located behind the wall).

THE FANS WHO MADE THE SHOW

In 1939, a baseball milestone was set at Ebbets, one that would have long-term repercussions but was little noted at the time. On August 26, 1939, the first big-league baseball game was televised. We can't say broadcast, since only about 100 TV sets existed close enough to pick up the signal. But the Reds-Dodgers game was on the air, and though it would not really pick up steam for another couple of decades, the march toward TV sports had begun.

It's also fun to note that the first football game to be televised was also played at Ebbets Field. The NFL's Brooklyn Dodgers, who played at Ebbets from 1930 to 1944, took on the visiting Philadelphia Eagles, and won 23–14. Skip Walz, the NBC reporter for the game, told the Pro Football Hall of Fame, "It was a cloudy day, when the sun crept behind the stadium there wasn't enough light for the cameras. The picture would get darker and darker, and eventually it would go completely blank, and we'd revert to a radio broadcast."

But back to baseball. Though their ballpark was now large and spacious and adorned with colorful ads, the fans found that the team on the field didn't measure up. No problem. Being colorful and creative Brooklynites, they set about making a game entertaining no matter what.

In fact, few fan bases were more loyal, colorful, and as intimately tied to their team as were the Brooklyn faithful. Beginning in the late 1930s and continuing until the end of Ebbets's run, the fans became a bigger part of the show. Their names are part of the baseball lexicon, in some circles as well known as the players they cheered for.

Albie the Truck Driver did not care for the underwhelming late-1920s teams and derided them all as "bums," a nickname that would not only stick, but be embraced, as "Da Bums" became the team's unofficial name. Even after being given a free pass to games in return for toning down his bummers, Albie refused it, preferring to both pay and heckle.

Jack Pierce so loved outfielder Cookie Lavagetto that he brayed a long and piercing (sorry for the pun) "Coooooookie!" to cheer his hero.

Hilda Chester sat in the center field bleachers, incessantly ringing her cowbell. Originally a stadium

Cowbells ringing, Hilda Chester cheered on her boys for decades, adding to the ballpark's legacy of colorful fans.

concession worker, she missed watching the games, so she installed herself and her bells in the outfield.

And though the ballpark had a famous organist in Gladys Gooding (please thank Gladys next time you hear the "Mexican Hat Dance" at a game), the musical talents (and we use the word loosely) of the Dodgers Sym-phony (rhymes with pony) had the most lasting effect on fans. Made up of a handful of musically deficient enthusiasts, at first they were a wildcat group sneaking in their instruments. By the late 1940s, however, team owners had given them permanent seats. So well known was the band and its antics that in 1951, a musicians' union complained that the boys were unpaid and complained to owner Walter O'Malley. Instead of agreeing to pay them (rumor was he did pay them a bit anyway), O'Malley opened up the whole ballpark

1949
WORLD SERIES
Ebbets Field — Brooklyn, N. Y.

EBBETS FIELD

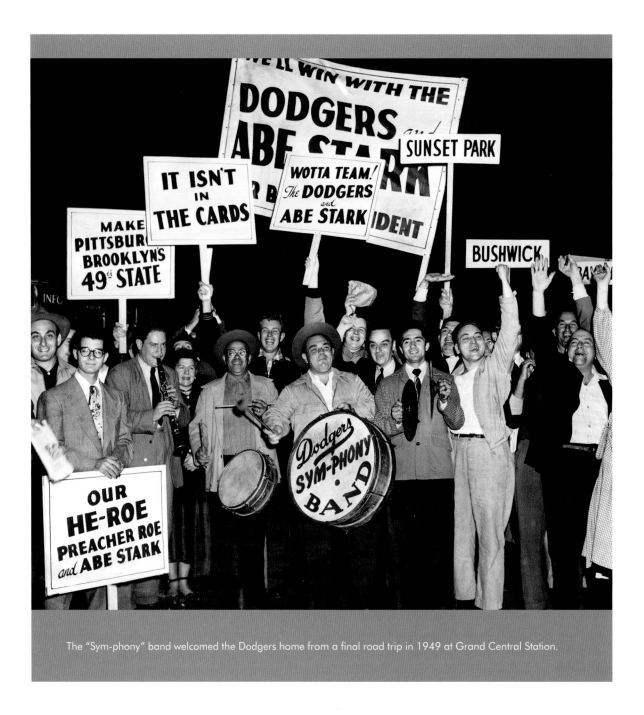

The "Sym-phony" band welcomed the Dodgers home from a final road trip in 1949 at Grand Central Station.

to instruments for "Music Appreciation Night." The union backed down.

As the band played on and the faithful followed faithfully, in 1941 the Dodgers rewarded their fans with a trip to the World Series against the Yankees, but it was an ill-fated one. The Dodgers trailed two games to one but were leading game 4 at Ebbets Field 4–3 in the ninth. They got the final strikeout of Tommy Henrich, but the third strike eluded Brooklyn backstop Mickey Owen. Still just one out from victory, the Dodgers imploded, allowing four runs in a game they lost. The Yankees closed the series out in five games.

A MAN OF COURAGE

A few years later, however, Brooklyn started a magical decade that cemented the team's place in the hearts of its fans and Ebbets Field as a place where baseball miracles happen.

The first and most important miracle came in 1947. Until that year, African Americans had been effectively, if not "officially," banned from the majors. Not since 1884 had a black player taken part in any American or National League game. Dodgers general manager Branch Rickey set about to change that fact, quietly researching top players from the Negro Leagues in search of one or a few who could make the move from a skills standpoint, but also from a PR point of view. In Rickey's famous phrase, he was looking for a man "with the courage not to fight back," knowing that any powerful response to the baiting, taunting, and cursing that would surely accompany that player around the league would play into the hands of segregationists.

In 1946, Rickey signed Jackie Robinson, a multisport star at UCLA and a former Army officer then playing with the Kansas City Monarchs. Robinson's college background, to say nothing of his splendid play, would work in Rickey's plan. The young player played for the Dodgers' minor-league team in Montreal in '46. Somewhat removed from the divisive American scene, though he did experience clear racism while at spring training in Florida, Robinson prepared for the big leap.

Accompanied by a flood of newspaper ink either supporting or condemning the action, Rickey signed Robinson to the Dodgers and installed him at first base to start the season. On April 15, 1947, in front of an Ebbets Field packed with fans, many of whom were African American, Robinson took the field and the vile color line was broken forever.

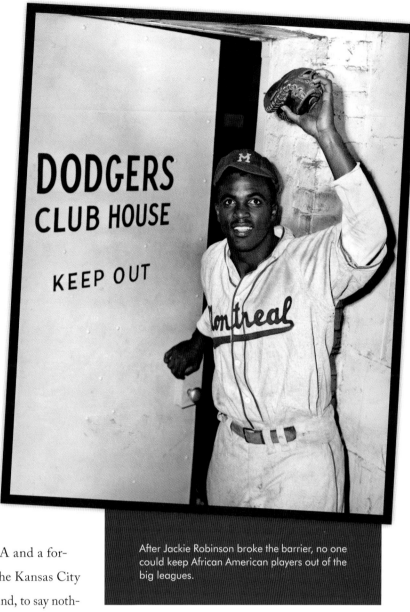

After Jackie Robinson broke the barrier, no one could keep African American players out of the big leagues.

Though some teammates grumbled, when captain Pee Wee Reese publicly embraced and supported his new first sacker, the grumbling stopped. At the same time, of course, players and fans alike were marveling at Robinson's speed on the base paths and hitting prowess. He was named the Rookie of the Year, an award that was later given his name.

With Robinson came the team's first N.L. pennant since 1941. Robinson started just about every game in 1947, though coming up alongside him were a few young players who would also have a big effect on Brooklyn in coming years, including Duke Snider

No StubHub or Ticketmaster in 1951: If you wanted a ticket to the big Dodgers-Giants playoff game in 1951, you stood in line outside Ebbets.

Shortstop and team captain Pee Wee Reese (second from left) helped smooth the path for his new teammate Jackie Robinson (right).

and Gil Hodges, to say nothing of 21-year-old pitcher Ralph Branca. However, 1947 also saw the Dodgers lose the first of four World Series in seven years, all to the New York Yankees. That year, the team lost in seven games. Over the next few years, the Subway Series was the toast of baseball, but the Yankees were just too good. "Wait till next year!" was the annual cry of Dodgers fans.

In 1951, the Dodgers lost a three-game series to that other New York ball club, the Giants, courtesy of Bobby Thomson's "Shot Heard 'Round the World."

In 1952 and 1953, they lost the World Series to the Yankees, and in 1954 finished second in the N.L. to—you guessed it—the Giants.

The Dodgers of the 1950s are the Dodgers that gave Ebbets and the borough a permanent place in baseball history. The team was packed with stars and with future Hall of Famers, but this being Brooklyn, everybody got a nickname anyway. "Pistol Pete" Reiser played right field. Harold Reese was short, so he was "Pee Wee." Carl Furillo had a great arm and was from a town in Pennsylvania, so he was the "Reading

The Ol' Redhead, Harold "Red" Barber came from down South, but found a welcoming home in Brooklyn. He later worked for the Yankees.

Rifle." And he loved scungilli, so he was also "Skoonj." Edwin Snider ruled the roost, so he was the "Duke of Flatbush." Roy Campanella was "Campy," Don Newcombe was "Newk." And of course Harry Arthur Lavagetto answered to "Cookie."

Of almost equal fun were the nicknames given players on visiting teams. It was in Brooklyn that the great Cardinals first baseman Stan Musial became "the Man," as in "here comes that man again." The distinctive ring of the famous Brooklyn accent provided a pair

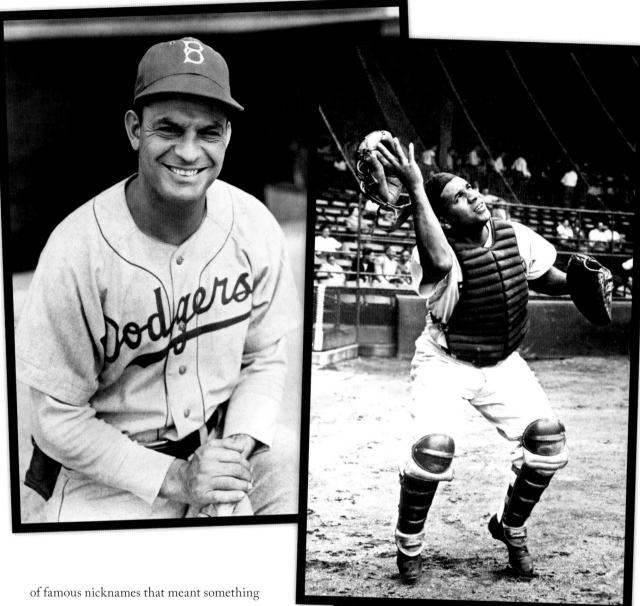

of famous nicknames that meant something quite different than most fans think. Paul and Lloyd Waner were "Big Poison" and "Little Poison," but it was not for their potentially deadly, toxin-like hitting. Rather, it was the Brooklyn fans' way of saying "big person" and "little person." (Go ahead, try to say it like a 1940s movie gangster . . . it works.)

And speaking of nicknames, one can't look back at the beloved Dodgers without a mention of their beloved radio and later TV announcer, Harold "Red" Barber. The gentlemanly Southerner with the corncob pipe full of country sayings called the games for the team from 1939 to 1953. A three-minute egg timer reminded "the

LEFT: Infielder Cookie Lavagetto played for Brooklyn from 1937–1941 and again in 1946–1947. In between he served four years in the armed forces in World War II.

ABOVE: Roy Campanella won three MVP awards in his 10-year Hall of Fame career, which was cut short after he was paralyzed in an auto accident in early 1958.

Ol' Redhead" to announce the score to radio listeners. In 1978, he was the first winner of the Ford Frick Award, given by the Baseball Hall of Fame in Cooperstown for excellence in broadcasting.

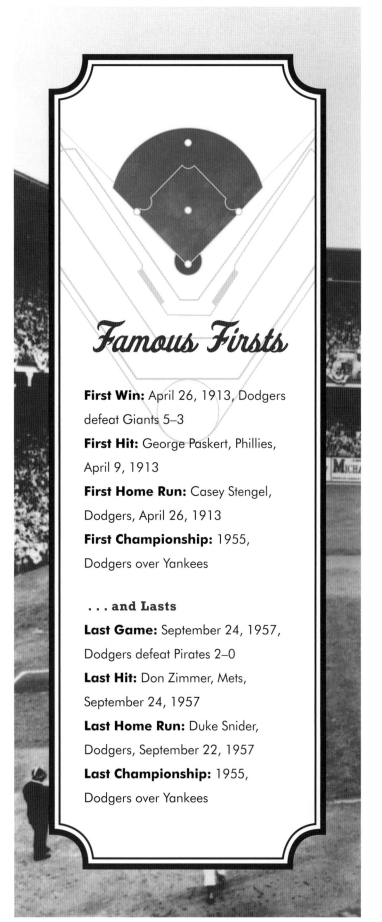

Famous Firsts

First Win: April 26, 1913, Dodgers defeat Giants 5–3

First Hit: George Paskert, Phillies, April 9, 1913

First Home Run: Casey Stengel, Dodgers, April 26, 1913

First Championship: 1955, Dodgers over Yankees

. . . and Lasts

Last Game: September 24, 1957, Dodgers defeat Pirates 2–0

Last Hit: Don Zimmer, Mets, September 24, 1957

Last Home Run: Duke Snider, Dodgers, September 22, 1957

Last Championship: 1955, Dodgers over Yankees

NEXT YEAR IS HERE

Finally, in 1955, for Charlie Ebbets, for Branch Rickey, for Casey Stengel, for all their long-suffering fans, the Dodgers finally came through. "Next year" finally came.

Brooklyn romped to the N.L. pennant, winning by 13½ games. They started out 22–2, including a season-opening 10-game winning streak. They boasted five future Hall of Famers in their lineup: Robinson, Snider, Hodges, Campanella, and Reese. They had a solid pitching staff led by Branca, Don Newcombe, and Carl Erskine (or, in Brooklynese, "Oy-skin"). Plus a kid named Sandy Koufax got in a dozen games for the club; he'd turn out to be a pretty good pitcher in L.A.

Seven times the Dodgers had made the World Series since moving into Ebbets Field. Seven times they had gone back to their homes in Brooklyn empty-handed. Then, in 1955, they lost the first two games to the Yankees. It looked very much like it was happening all over again.

Game 3 pitted young Johnny Podres, the only Dodgers starter with a losing record in 1955, against the Yankees' 17-game winner, Bob Turley. But the Bums were back home in Brooklyn and they won 8–3. In game 4, Campy, Hodges, and the Duke smacked homers and Brooklyn evened the series with an 8–5 win. Then they made it three straight in their home borough with a 5–3 win, led by a pair of Snider homers.

In game 6, back in the Bronx, the Yankees man-handled young starter Karl Spooner, scoring all of their five runs in the first inning. The Dodgers had no answer against Yankees ace Whitey Ford, who allowed only four hits, and the series came down to a seventh and deciding game in Yankee Stadium.

In game 7, Brooklyn went ahead 2–0 behind Podres. Then they got another Dodgers miracle. In the bottom of the sixth, left fielder Sandy Amoros raced to the

★

ABOVE: Compare this 1955 World Series crowd to earlier ballpark shots . . . hats, it seems, were starting to die out by the mid-'50s.

ENCLOSED 1: In this cigarette card of the 1913 Brooklyn team, note the old spelling of "Stengle," the presence of the mascots at far left and far right, and the face of team hero Zach Wheat, sixth from left in second row.

ENCLOSED 2: A pair of Hall of Fame managers grace the cover of the 1955 World Series program. Walter Alston of the Dodgers (bottom) led his team over Casey Stengel's Yankees in seven games.

Only at
EBBETS FIELD

★ ★ ★

- The right field wall had an ad from Abe Stark Clothiers that read "Hit Sign. Win Suit." The Dodgers' Woody English was so rewarded for his 1937 blast.

- The "chandelier" inside the entrance rotunda was made of baseball bats.

- The visitor's bullpen home plate was painted yellow.

left field line to make a one-handed snag of a drive by Yogi Berra. Amoros turned it into a double play and saved the game.

The tense, low-scoring game carried into the ninth. With all of Brooklyn holding its collective breath, Podres got the Yankees 1-2-3 and that was it.

The Brooklyn Dodgers were baseball's best. Whoda thunk it? Da Bums was da woild champs! It was the only World Series title that the Dodgers would earn while playing in Ebbets Field.

GOOD-BYE, BROOKLYN

But talk about your last hurrahs. Even as Brooklynites finally tasted the sweet champagne of victory, they were about to get a full-on dose of bile.

First, they lost the 1956 World Series to the Yankees, with the added ignominy of being the only team to have

a perfect game thrown against them (by Don Larsen at Yankee Stadium in game 5).

Then, Dodgers owner Walter O'Malley started to hatch a bold plan for his club, and he sprung it on the disbelieving public on October 8, 1957. (His first plan, for a domed stadium to be built at the prominent inter- section of Atlantic Avenue and Flatbush Avenue, was vetoed by the city's all-powerful parks commissioner, Robert Moses.) As O'Malley said on April 9, 1957, in a meeting with newspaper publishers, "We will play our schedule of games somewhere. I will continue down the road toward that ballpark until I reach a fork in the road. At that time I must decide which road to take, leading toward Los Angeles or to the new park in Brooklyn."

O'Malley was sure enough of his eventual move that he had plans made to play baseball at the L.A. Coliseum, since there was not a large-enough ballpark

in L.A. (yet!). He played some 1957 home games in Jersey City just to show Brooklyn city fathers what it would be like without the team.

Spurred by both the slowly fading Ebbets Field, the changing character of the neighborhood (especially after trolley service ended in 1956), and wooed by an amazing offer from the West Coast, O'Malley had been planning the move for a while. He bought a team airplane in early 1957 (a Corvair 440 Metropolitan DC-3). He had moved the team's top minor-league club

TOP: Duke Snider (4) moves to the plate to greet Sandy Amoros, who is about to score following a bases-loaded walk to Pee Wee Reese, who makes his own way to first base in game 3 of the 1955 World Series.

ABOVE: In game 4 of the same series, Amoros scored again, this time on a double by Junior Gilliam. Yogi Berra's tag was too late, while Reese watches.

TOP: By early 1960, the wreckers had moved in to demolish Ebbets Field.

ABOVE: A drawn-out plan by the Dodgers to move was opposed by city and state officials—as well as by these young ballplayers—but O'Malley made the move after the 1957 season.

from Fort Worth to L.A. that year, too. Numerous visits with L.A. officials and promises of land and favorable local deals made it a no-brainer. O'Malley got the Giants together with San Francisco and that New York club announced its move in August. The N.L. had given its approval for a two-team move in May. A domed stadium proposal for Brooklyn died a quick death. Even a last-ditch effort by financier and future New York governor Nelson Rockefeller could not stop the move.

The team that was among the most dearly beloved was giving its sweethearts the brush-off.

The final game turned out to be September 24, 1957, with the Dodgers beating the Pirates 2–0. Fewer than 10,000 fans showed up to say good-bye, perhaps not believing that it was really true. News reports had

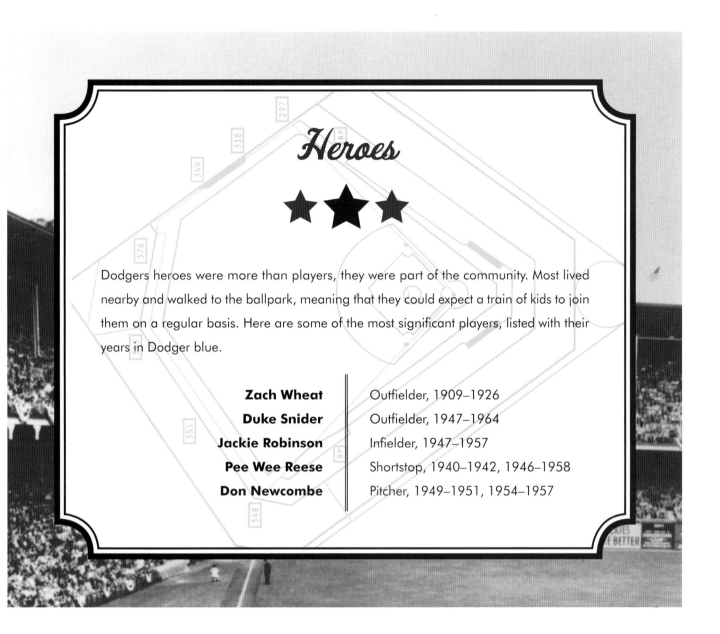

Heroes

★ ★ ★

Dodgers heroes were more than players, they were part of the community. Most lived nearby and walked to the ballpark, meaning that they could expect a train of kids to join them on a regular basis. Here are some of the most significant players, listed with their years in Dodger blue.

Zach Wheat	Outfielder, 1909–1926
Duke Snider	Outfielder, 1947–1964
Jackie Robinson	Infielder, 1947–1957
Pee Wee Reese	Shortstop, 1940–1942, 1946–1958
Don Newcombe	Pitcher, 1949–1951, 1954–1957

followed O'Malley's decision making throughout the summer, but he did not make the move official until October 8. There would be no good-bye ceremony for the ball club or the ballpark. Not with a bang, but a whimper. However, this muted departure grew steadily to a drumbeat of anger over the years, as Brooklynites pointed to the departure of Da Bums as the death knell for their borough's legendary sense of community and independence. To this day, you can find hardy old borough residents who will loudly proclaim that "da place ain't bin da same since." Maybe it was the Dodgers' perennial bridesmaid status, maybe it was the feeling of the entire borough always in the shadow of next-door Manhattan, but in either case, losing the

Dodgers came to define the difference between what was and what Brooklyn has become.

Ebbets Field itself had no baseball life after the Dodgers left, unlike the Polo Grounds, which at least saw the Mets start out. The home of Hilda Chester, Albie the Truck Driver, Pee Wee, the Duke, and so many others fell. It was replaced by a housing project.

No one has played baseball there since 1957, but you can still meet old-timers who remember ol' Ebbets Field like it was yesterday, a special place filled with special people.

Somewhere in this crowd outside Wrigley Field before a 1945 World Series game is a man with a goat. The animal didn't get into the ballpark, he cursed the team, and the Cubs haven't won since. Gotta love Wrigley . . .

CHAPTER SIX

WRIGLEY FIELD

CHICAGO, ILL.

YEAR BUILT	1914
HOME TEAMS	Chicago Whales, Chicago Cubs
FIRST GAME	April 23, 1914 (Whales); April 20, 1916 (Cubs)
CAPACITY (AVERAGE)	39,000
FAMOUS FEATURES	Ivy-covered outfield walls, vocal bleacher fans, wildcat seats on nearby buildings, Wrigleyville neighborhood

The Friendly Confines": How perfect is Wrigley Field's nickname? In that simple phrase, whether you've been to a game there or not, you're transported to that brick-and-ivy ballpark, nestled amid the hustle and bustle of a part of a big city that even has its own name, "Wrigleyville."

Friendly? Welcome to our home, say the fans. It's a place where everybody knows your name, as long as you're not wearing Cardinals or White Sox gear. They play most of their games in the daytime, for goodness' sake! It's like 1940 every day.

TOP: The simple curve of the roofline belies the complex relationship that Wrigley has with its neighborhood; notice the apartment buildings along Waveland Avenue to the bottom right.

ABOVE: Even as the ballpark has had some minor renovations inside and out, the classic neon sign remains. The hand-operated lower part has gone electric, of course, but it's still the place where locals check on upcoming games.

Confines? Sounds constricting, but in this case, it means enveloping, enwrapping, enfolding. You step onto the block where the ballpark sits, you check out the big red sign out front—"Game Today," it reads. You pass inside the bricks and you're in another place and time, you're gathered in with a million memories. Wrigley retains its special place in the hearts of baseball fans for its timelessness, its connection to a beloved past even while making new memories (okay, not always good ones) each season. Like Fenway Park, it remains a real-life touchstone on the continuum of the game, a time machine wrapped in ivy. And to think it all started with egg creams and five-cent sandwiches.

Cubs fans can thank Lucky Charlie Weeghman for putting what would become Wrigley Field in place, though originally the field was for a Federal League team.

A BALLPARK BUILT WITH COFFEE

Of all the ballparks featured in our book, Wrigley is the only one not originally built for a Major League team. The Cubs, of course, had been part of the National League since 1876, but they didn't really have a permanent home, playing most of their games at DePaul University's diamond. The A.L.'s White Sox were the big draw in town, especially after noted skinflint Charles Comiskey pried open his wallet to build Comiskey Park on the South Side in 1909.

Enter into the saga of Chicago baseball one "Lucky Charlie," Charles Weeghman. A hustler from the word go, Weeghman started his business career as a waiter,

soon owned the joint, and expanded to create a chain of luncheonettes. His timing was perfect, as Chicago, like other big American cities, was fast becoming a place where millions worked and lived. The farms were shrinking, and city jobs didn't leave time to amble back to the bunkhouse for chow. A quick bite and then back to work, young man, all thanks to Weeghman's.

At the same time that Weeghman's was expanding, baseball was booming. Attendance from 1903 to 1908 more than tripled. Other businesspeople wanted in, but after having trouble buying into the American or National Leagues, a group of them headed by "Fighting Jim" Gilmore started a third pro baseball organization. The eight-team Federal League was set for debut in 1914, including four teams in cities that already had Major League clubs. But Gilmore needed a Chicago partner, a man with deep pockets and guts. He found his man in Lucky Charlie, who bought the Chitown franchise in the new league. In a town with two pro baseball teams (the Cubs and White Stockings), Weeghman felt there was room for one more, and he bought in as owner of the Whales. But the Whales needed a place to play.

On the home of the former Chicago Lutheran Theological Seminary, on Chicago's North Side, he found the site. The North Side was actually a very unusual choice. The bulk of the city's residents lived on the South Side, where Comiskey Park was located. Imagine someone in Los Angeles today building in the far northern San Fernando Valley or in New York thinking that a stadium in Far Rockaway was the right move. The North Side was virgin territory. *Chicago Tribune* columnist Ring Lardner claimed on opening day of the new ballpark that "many of our citizens will today visit the North Side for the first time." However, thanks to the newfangled car and expanding public transportation—a model seen in a burgeoning New

Top 10 Moments at
WRIGLEY FIELD

★ ★ ★

(in chronological order)

May 2, 1917

The only double no-hit game (sort of) ever pitched is thrown at Wrigley Field by the Cubs' Hippo Vaughn and the Reds' Fred Toney. Neither pitcher allows a hit for nine innings; Cincy's Jim Thorpe breaks it up with a homer in the 10th to win it.

October 1, 1932

Babe Ruth's "called shot" in game 3 of the World Series.

October 10, 1945

The Cubs lose to Detroit in their final World Series appearance (through 2012).

May 12, 1970

Ernie Banks, "Mr. Cub," hits his 500th career homer on the way to a total of 512.

August 9, 1988

The first official night game is played at Wrigley Field.

July 10, 1990

The first nighttime All-Star Game in Wrigley history is won by the A.L., 2–0.

April 4, 1994

Cubs rookie Tuffy Rhodes hits three solo homers on opening day, but the Cubs lose, 12–8. He ends up with eight for the whole season.

May 6, 1998

Cubs rookie Kerry Wood ties a single-game record by striking out 20 Houston Astros.

October 14, 2003

A fan interferes with a Cubs outfielder during an NLCS game. Following the missed out, the Cubs lose the game.

January 1, 2009

An NHL game is played on a rink constructed on Wrigley's diamond. The Red Wings beat the Blackhawks, 6–4.

When crowds at Weeghman got too large for the stands to handle, temporary bleachers were installed at the foul lines and in the outfield—standing room only.

York and even an expanding Boston—reaching what was heretofore the outskirts of a city became much easier. Weeghman, in fact, was prescient in his choice, seeing what was happening to his own American city and setting himself and his ball club up to benefit.

Using a model loosely based on the Polo Grounds, architect Zachary Taylor Davis designed the ballpark at 1060 W. Addison, an address as familiar to Chicagoans as 161st and River Avenue is to New Yorkers or Yawkey

Way is to Bostonians. Weeghman spent $250,000 on the ballpark he called Weeghman Field, which would hold 14,000 people for the 1914 season. The park had a single deck of seats from foul pole to foul pole, with a wide walkway between two sections of seats, one behind the other. For big games, bleachers were put on the edges of the outfield or along the far edges of the left and right field lines, shrinking the field a bit. The brick exterior was part of the design from the start, but the

Day One

"Chicago took the Federal League to its bosom yesterday and claimed it as a mother would claim a long-lost child. With more frills and enthusiasm than ever prevailed at a baseball opening here, Joe Tinker and his Chifeds made their debut before a throng of fans that filled the new north side park to capacity . . ."

Chicago Tribune, April 24, 1914

walking in front of them, blocking the view. So his ballpark became the first to establish fixed concession stands. Fans could get their food and head back to their seats, just as generations have done since. So blame Lucky Charlie next time you miss a home run standing in line for a beer. Another fan-friendly innovation he added seems stunningly obvious but was not accepted baseball-wide until 1923: letting fans keep the foul balls that went into the stands. Until Weeghman's decision, clubs demanded the balls back, sometimes even sending security guards to fight with fans for the precious orbs.

HERE COME THE CUBBIES

North Side or no, and with fan-friendly ideas like that, the new park was a hit. Opening day, April 23, was overflowing, with thousands shut out of the gates due to overcrowding. A pregame "bullfight" on the field fizzled, but the huge American flag carried by the Daughters of the Grand Army of the Republic was well received, as were the scads of flowers presented to players and owner. Weeghman's new team continued to pack them in all season, outdrawing the White Sox and Cubs by 10-to-1 each by the end of the 1914 campaign. Did those early Chicago fans know already what a good thing they had there on Addison?

However, as popular as the Chicago team was, the entire Federal League struggled to keep players, as the majors battled back to retain their top stars in the bidding war. The Whales surfaced for only one more season, 1915, after which the Federal League took the deep dive. But Weeghman's park was such a hit and National League owners so envied its success that he was allowed the chance to buy the Cubs. And just like that, the Cubs and what would be Wrigley Field were married on April 23, 1916.

brick outfield walls came later. The single-deck design did not have too many architectural flourishes, but the high walls behind home plate on the outside would later prove to be the perfect spot for an iconic sign.

Inside the park, Weeghman, with his understanding of the importance of making a customer happy, found that people didn't like having all the vendors constantly

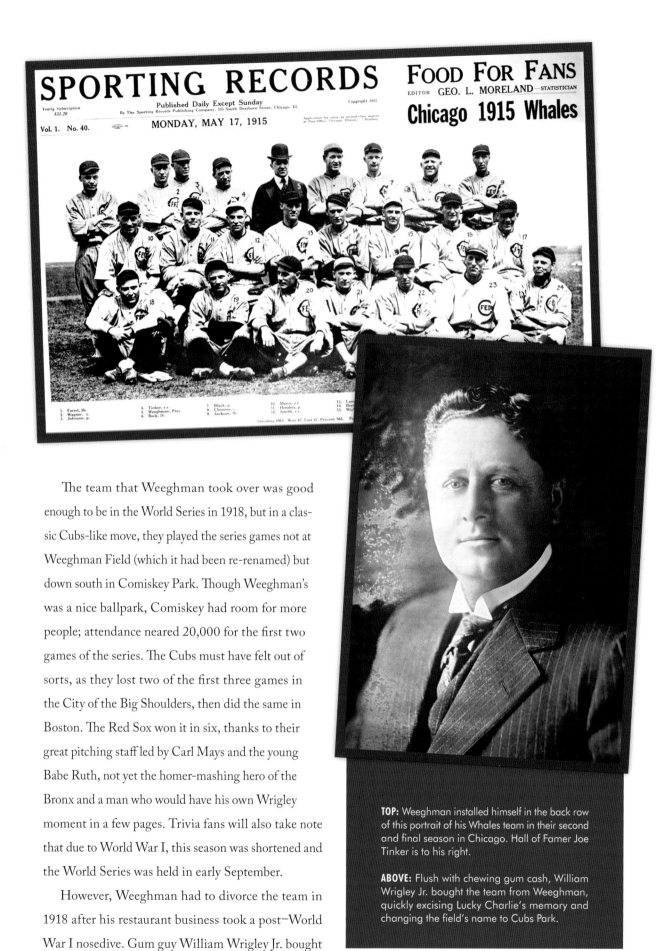

SPORTING RECORDS

FOOD FOR FANS
EDITOR GEO. L. MORELAND — STATISTICIAN

Chicago 1915 Whales

Published Daily Except Sunday
Yearly Subscription
$31.20
By The Sporting Records Publishing Company, 333 South Dearborn Street, Chicago, Ill.
Copyright 1915

Vol. 1. No. 40.   MONDAY, MAY 17, 1915   Application for entry as second-class matter at Post-Office, Chicago, Illinois. Pending

The team that Weeghman took over was good enough to be in the World Series in 1918, but in a classic Cubs-like move, they played the series games not at Weeghman Field (which it had been re-renamed) but down south in Comiskey Park. Though Weeghman's was a nice ballpark, Comiskey had room for more people; attendance neared 20,000 for the first two games of the series. The Cubs must have felt out of sorts, as they lost two of the first three games in the City of the Big Shoulders, then did the same in Boston. The Red Sox won it in six, thanks to their great pitching staff led by Carl Mays and the young Babe Ruth, not yet the homer-mashing hero of the Bronx and a man who would have his own Wrigley moment in a few pages. Trivia fans will also take note that due to World War I, this season was shortened and the World Series was held in early September.

However, Weeghman had to divorce the team in 1918 after his restaurant business took a post–World War I nosedive. Gum guy William Wrigley Jr. bought

TOP: Weeghman installed himself in the back row of this portrait of his Whales team in their second and final season in Chicago. Hall of Famer Joe Tinker is to his right.

ABOVE: Flush with chewing gum cash, William Wrigley Jr. bought the team from Weeghman, quickly excising Lucky Charlie's memory and changing the field's name to Cubs Park.

BASE
BALL
WRIGLEY
FIELD
TODAY

Hall of Famer Rogers Hornsby (top left) highlights this photo of the 1929 Cubbies, by then owned by Wrigley (center) and with the original Bill Veeck as president.

the team. He made it his mission to make it a special place. As he later said, after numerous improvements, "I spent $2,300,000 to make Wrigley Field clean, convenient, comfortable, and attractive to the eye. The effect of these improved surroundings upon baseball patrons has been remarkable."

Imagine, an owner making improvements so that fans have more fun, not spend more money. Under Wrigley, the park, which was renamed Cubs Park, went through some big changes in the ensuing years. The biggest came in 1922, when the entire diamond was shifted 20 yards southwest to alleviate some problems with the sun in batters' eyes and also to create room for more seating. Today's pitcher's mound is the home plate of 1919. In 1926, the ballpark made one of its biggest and most important changes: It got yet another new name, but this one would stick—Wrigley Field. It also got bigger. During that off-season, Wrigley added double-decking all around the diamond, save for the single deck of bleachers above the outfield walls. Capacity increased to 38,000 people, up from 18,000. Wrigley Field now looked essentially like the Wrigley Field you see today.

When a modern fan walks into the ballpark, his vista (save for some of the ads and the clothing around him) is not unlike what his grandfather saw and what his father witnessed. That immutability is a big part of the nostalgic appeal of Wrigley. Fans get that sense of history, that sense of "on this spot . . ." and it's not just a brass marker—it's the actual place. As nice as today's new ballparks are, and for all that they try to borrow from these jewel boxes, they'll never have the history.

NEW TENANTS AND SAME OLD CUBS

The 1920s also saw the arrival of new autumn tenants for Wrigley Field. The NFL's Chicago Bears arrived in 1922 and played their homes games in Wrigley until 1970. The Bears first played as the Staleys, their name back in Decatur, but they changed to Bears to mirror the Cubbies. The team won the first-ever official NFL Championship Game at Wrigley in 1933, giving them the second of seven NFL titles they would win while Wrigley residents. Led by "Papa Bear" George Halas, the Bears were an NFL force for decades. Red Grange

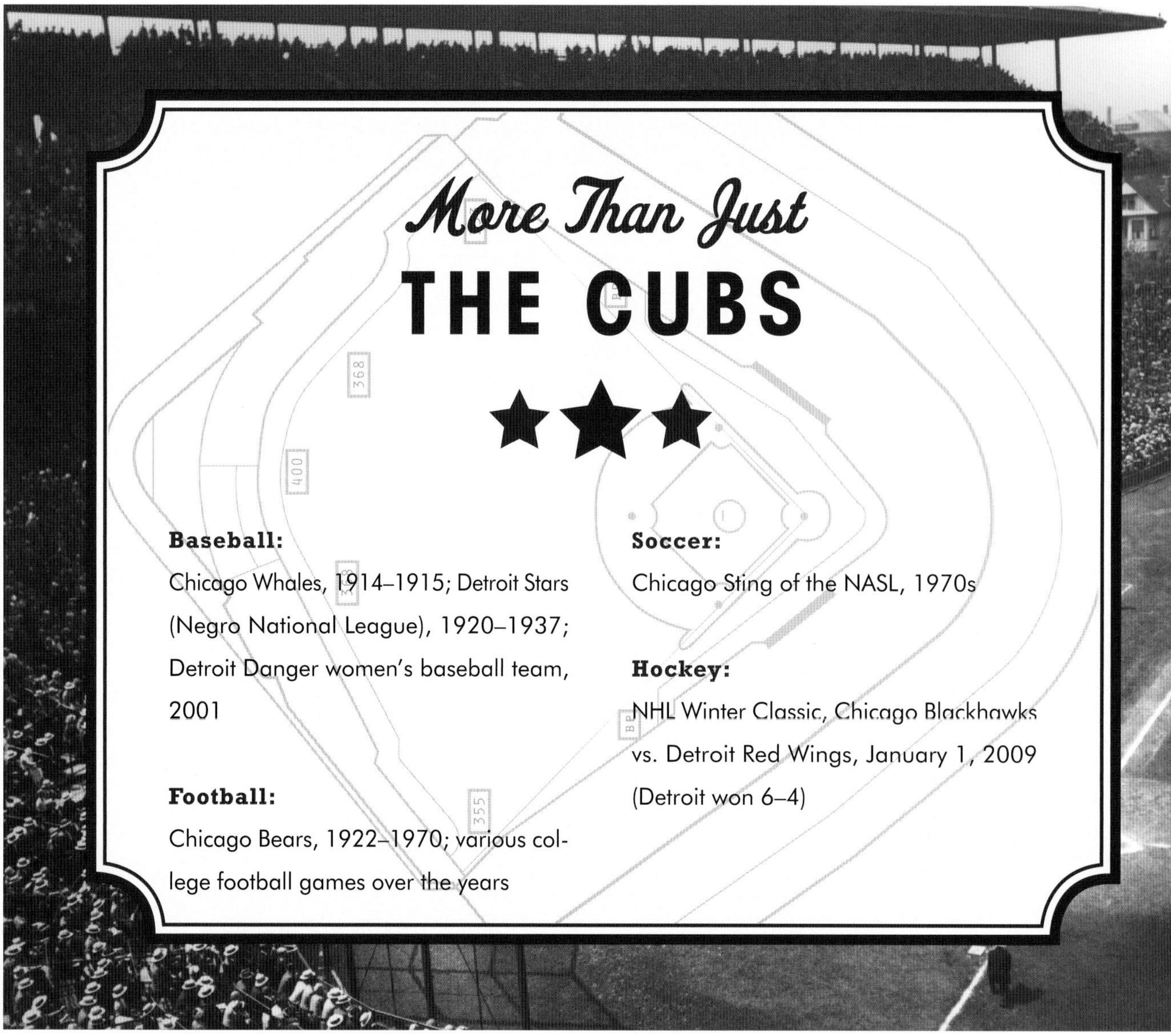

More Than Just
THE CUBS
★ ★ ★

Baseball:

Chicago Whales, 1914–1915; Detroit Stars (Negro National League), 1920–1937; Detroit Danger women's baseball team, 2001

Football:

Chicago Bears, 1922–1970; various college football games over the years

Soccer:

Chicago Sting of the NASL, 1970s

Hockey:

NHL Winter Classic, Chicago Blackhawks vs. Detroit Red Wings, January 1, 2009 (Detroit won 6–4)

galloped here, Sid Luckman passed his way into the record books, Gale Sayers romped. Dick Butkus made his first tackles for "Da Bears" in Wrigley Field. A 14–10 win at Wrigley over the New York Giants in 1963 was the last title the Bears would win on the North Side.

But back to baseball: All those new seats at the expanded Wrigley came in handy in 1929 when the World Series returned to Chicago. This time, the Cubs would play at their own ballpark. As would become a theme throughout the life of Wrigley Field, the Cubs choked. They lost the first two games of the series to Philadelphia in the Friendly Confines (the roots of that famous nickname, by the way, are hotly disputed, though Hall of Famer Ernie Banks gets credit for

making it popular). They won game 3 but then pulled a real Cubbie in game 4. Ahead 8–0, they somehow allowed the Athletics to score 10 runs in the bottom of the seventh. Three A's hitters, including Hall of Famers Jimmie Foxx and Al Simmons, had two hits in the inning. Then Chicago did it again in game 5. With a two-run lead in the ninth, the Cubs gave up a two-run homer to Mule Haas and a game-winning single to Bing Miller. Game, set, and series.

The Cubs got another chance at World Series glory in 1932, but again it was the opponent who made history. Their nemesis from 1918, Ruth, was now a Yankees slugger, and he led the Bronx Bombers into Wrigley for game 3. New York had won the first two games in

When the Cubs traveled to Philly for games during the 1929 World Series, fans put on their hats and stood in the Loop to watch the action unfold on the "Play-o-Gram" board (top left).

Yankee Stadium. Meanwhile, Ruth had given Cubs fans another reason to dislike him, having bad-mouthed the Cubs for how the team treated former Yankee Mark Koenig, a part-timer for Chicago in 1932. The Wrigley faithful, along with their chirping dugout, were ready for Ruth and laid into him as he came to the plate in game 3 with the score tied 4–4 (Ruth's three-run shot in the first having started the scoring).

Cubs pitcher Charlie Root got in a called strike to start the at-bat. On 2–1, Root put another strike by Ruth. Then history happened . . . or not, depending on your point of view. The legend says that Ruth, in response to the rising chorus of taunts, raised his hand and pointed to center field, to the bleachers far behind Root. Fact is hazy on the subject of whether he pointed to center, gestured to the Cubs bench, or just raised his hand in acknowledgment of the strike call. Both legend and fact agree on what happened next, however: Ruth smashed the next pitch he saw into those same center field seats for what proved to be the winning run. As he jogged the bases, he tipped his cap to the enraged fans. Did Ruth "call" his shot? He did or didn't depending on which team you cheer for.

THE PLANTING OF THE IVY

William Wrigley was not around to watch whether Ruth did or didn't. He died before the 1932 season and his son Philip took over the team. In the late 1930s, the Wrigley scion added some of the sparkle that made Wrigley Field what it is today. The famous scoreboard, topped with its mighty round clockface and adorned with N.L. team flags, was first used in 1937. The iconic scoreboard has remained ever since as one of the park's most distinctive parts. It's one of only two hand-operated boards in the bigs, the other being on Fenway's Green Monster.

Charlie Root gave up Babe Ruth's famous "called shot" in the 1932 series. Root was about halfway through a fine 16-year run with the Cubbies.

The other icon isn't there all the time, but when it's growing, it truly sets Wrigley Field apart from all other ballparks. In 1937, Wrigley asked team executive Bill Veeck to add some greenery to the field. Their first attempt, a row of trees set atop the outfield walls, lasted mere days in the mighty wind off Lake Michigan, a few blocks away. (How bad was the wind at Wrigley? Its direction defines the action. The best example came in 1922, when the Cubs beat the Phillies 26–23, the most runs ever scored in a big-league game. Or a game in 1979 when 11 homers jumped into the jet stream that roared over Wrigley.) Their next horticultural try proved more fruitful, so to speak. Veeck ordered 350 pots of Japanese bittersweet and 200 pots of Boston ivy

planted along the edges of the brick outfield wall. Over time, the ivy grew to cover the walls and each spring as it renews, it brings with it the distinctive green-and-red look that is Wrigley.

The Cubs lost the World Series again in 1935 against the Tigers, even after Detroit lost slugger Hank Greenberg a game-plus into the series. In 1938, they were swept by the Cincinnati Reds. (The Cubs had earned the N.L. pennant, however, on a signature Wrigley moment. With the league title on the line, the Cubs beat the Pirates in late September when catcher Gabby Hartnett hit a homer in the falling twilight. It seemed to go out, but legend has it that friendly fans made sure to snag it and pull it into the bleachers. Thus the legendary "Homer in the Gloamin'.")

In 1945, the Cubs made it seven World Series losses in a row. However, this time the cause was partly supernatural (according to legend). Supposedly, a Greek restaurant owner named Billy Sianis brought his pet

TOP: The hand-operated scoreboard kept fans abreast of developments around the league; scores were sent first by telegraph, then phone, and now by the Internet. Note the Cubs and White Sox games set off by the horizontal lines midway down.

ABOVE: A rare shot of Wrigley Field's brick walls, this shows workers planting the famous ivy at the behest of Bill Veeck.

★ ★

The smile that launched
a thousand (mythical)
doubleheaders: Ernie
Banks rightly earned the
nickname "Mr. Cub" in
his 19-year Hall of Fame
career in Chicago.

★

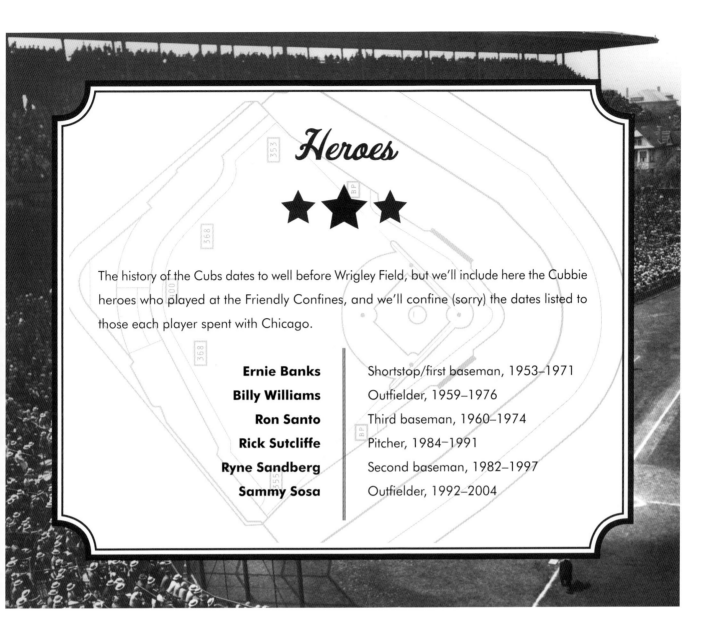

Heroes

★ ★ ★

The history of the Cubs dates to well before Wrigley Field, but we'll include here the Cubbie heroes who played at the Friendly Confines, and we'll confine (sorry) the dates listed to those each player spent with Chicago.

Ernie Banks	Shortstop/first baseman, 1953–1971
Billy Williams	Outfielder, 1959–1976
Ron Santo	Third baseman, 1960–1974
Rick Sutcliffe	Pitcher, 1984–1991
Ryne Sandberg	Second baseman, 1982–1997
Sammy Sosa	Outfielder, 1992–2004

goat to the game for good luck. When the animal was refused entry (Why? According to the version of the legend told by the Billy Goat Tavern's current site, Philip Wrigley said at the time, "Because the goat stinks."), Sianis put a curse on the team. The "Billy Goat Curse" would come up often in the ensuing decades as Cubs fans saw their beloved team jinxed again and again. In 1945, however, billy goat or no, the Cubs gave up five runs in the first inning of game 5—at Wrigley!—and that had more to do with losing than any hoodoo that he did.

Or did it? The Cubs wouldn't return to the postseason for almost 40 years (and as of this writing still have not won a World Series since 1908). Most of those years were spent in or near the N.L. cellar. As wonderful as Wrigley Field was, the whole point of going was to watch the Cubs and hope they won. With that hope so often dashed, attendance plummeted. The team didn't draw even one million fans any year from 1953 through 1967. There were bright spots on the field, however. A lanky shortstop (later first baseman) named Ernie Banks brought a home-run swing and a million-dollar smile to the North Side. He was named the N.L. MVP in 1958 and 1959, the first player from a last-place team to earn those honors. He eventually became known as Mr. Cub and one of the nicest people in baseball. His famous cry of "It's such a nice day, let's play two," is still used by Little League coaches to extol the joy of the game for young players.

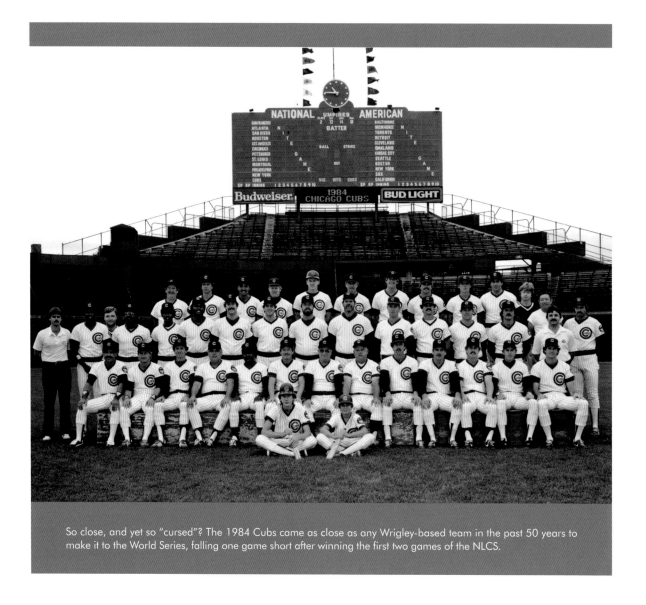

So close, and yet so "cursed"? The 1984 Cubs came as close as any Wrigley-based team in the past 50 years to make it to the World Series, falling one game short after winning the first two games of the NLCS.

Banks was on the back end of his Hall of Fame career when he got some help in the late 1960s. A trio of future Hall of Famers—outfielder Billy Williams, third baseman Ron Santo, and pitcher Ferguson Jenkins—helped Banks lead the Cubs to their best season in, well . . . decades. In 1969, they led the newly formed N.L. East by nine games in mid-August. By early September, they were barely holding on. Then an eight-game losing streak (part of a nasty 4–14 run) doomed their chances once again.

The Wrigley family sold the Cubs to the Tribune Company in 1981 for $20.5 million. The Trib got a bargain in part because the players had gone on strike. On strike or not, none of those players could say they had ever played a night game at Wrigley. Though lights

had been in ballparks since 1938 and every other park was lit by 1948, the Cubbies stubbornly resisted. An oft-told tale is that they did break down before the 1942 season, but the steel for the light towers was donated to the war effort.

In 1984, the Cubs made the N.L. Championship Series. But that meant day games in the playoffs, which TV hated. And if they'd made it to the World Series . . . gasp! There goes our TV money! To forestall this possibility, MLB sent a clear message: Turn on the lights. (The Cubs helped out, of course, by choking away the N.L. Championship Series. After winning the first two games at Wrigley, they flew to San Diego and lost three straight and the series. Was it the goat again?)

Hard to say who had more fun at a ball game than Harry Caray, who blared out the good and the bad about the Cubbies from 1982 to 1997.

But the lighting debate raged on after the season. The main objections were from the neighborhood, which didn't want looming light towers or to have their evenings turned to daytime. They also didn't want the crowds in their front yards at night. The team was also enjoying its iconoclastic status as the lone holdout; day baseball in Chicago was sort of a team trademark. Legislators bloviated, local fans rallied and sued, but eventually the modern age won out (especially after Major League owners gave the park an All-Star Game on condition that it have lights). The city council voted its okay immediately, passing an ordinance allowing night baseball there (though on a limited basis).

The first game was going to be played on the numerically propitious 8-8-88, but rain cut the game short. The next night the first official, full night game ever at

Wrigley Field was played. The Cubs actually won, too, beating the Mets 6–4.

HOLY COW! HERE COMES HARRY!

The floodlights were not the only things shining attention on Wrigley Field. The Tribune's WGN station began carrying the games nationwide. In 1982, they had gotten a television host worthy of their beloved ballpark. Harry Caray was already a legendary broadcaster for his 24 years with the Cardinals and 10 with the White Sox. Lured to Wrigley, he was instantly the team's most famous personality. His enormous glasses,

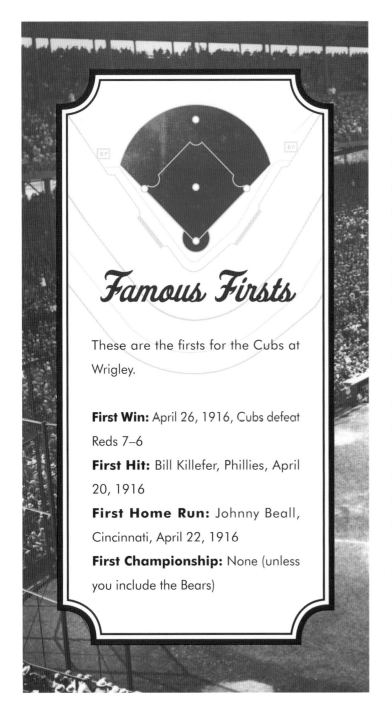

Famous Firsts

These are the firsts for the Cubs at Wrigley.

First Win: April 26, 1916, Cubs defeat Reds 7–6

First Hit: Bill Killefer, Phillies, April 20, 1916

First Home Run: Johnny Beall, Cincinnati, April 22, 1916

First Championship: None (unless you include the Bears)

that even inspired a stage play of the same name that continues to be revived around the country. As much as Wrigley was known for its ivy, it became more and more known as an amazing place to see a ball game, as much for the people and the surroundings as for the actual game. People started to make pilgrimages to the ballpark. Summer vacations were planned around being part of the game-day atmosphere. Singing with Harry, tossing opposing home runs back on the field, watching the wind play havoc with flying baseballs . . . everyone, it seemed, wanted to be part of the fun. Even the Cubs losing was almost part of the act. Shared suffering merged with shared joy at the ballpark to create a fan experience unique in baseball.

In 1987, the Cubs topped two million fans in attendance for the first time, and they've been above that almost ever since (in fact they now top three million a year regularly). Along with lights and Harry, the 1984 team and some that followed it helped, too. With stars like Ryne Sandberg and Andre Dawson, pitchers like Rick Sutcliffe and Greg Maddux, the team had players known nationally to go with their nationally known ballpark. Sandberg was the first second baseman to lead the league in homers (40 in 1990). Outfielder Dawson was the MVP in 1987, the first player from a last-place team to win the award since Ernie Banks. Maddux won the Cy Young Award in 1992, then left for the Braves, where he won three more Cy Youngs.

In the 1980s, as the Cubs had some decent teams and Caray was blaring his well-loved blather, WGN began satellite broadcasting games nationwide. Chicago celebrities also jumped in to spread the word, and Wrigley underwent a bit of a renaissance. (Actor Bill Murray was just one of a pack of Chicagoans who made their love of the Cubs known worldwide.) After suffering through some tough decades, Cubs fans seemed to have earned

booming voice ("Cubs win! Cubs win! Cubs win!"), and his seventh-inning singing of "Take Me Out to the Ballgame" all contributed to his becoming the face and voice of the Cubs.

His everyman personality—he seemed like a guy you could have a beer with, day or night—made him fit right in with what was becoming the defining part of Wrigley Field's fans: the Bleacher Bums. A group of regulars soon established base camp in left field, creating an atmosphere of conviviality and baseball-lovin'

the respect of the baseball world for sticking through it, and in Wrigley, they had their fortress.

And then came Sammy.

SOSA THE SLUGGER

The mighty blasts and happy hops of Sammy Sosa, an outfielder who joined the Cubs in 1992, brought even more attention to Wrigley. Though he was a potent home-run threat for his first few years in Chicago, in 1998, for whatever reason (insert your own opinions here, bleacher bums), he started hitting homers at a record pace. In fact, Sosa's home-run race with Cardinals first baseman Mark McGwire that summer thrilled all of baseball, especially the fans at Wrigley. Whether or not time and the specter of performance-enhancing drugs has dimmed the memories, anyone who lived through that countdown summer of '98 will never forget the pounding thrill of each Sosa at-bat at Wrigley. Would he hit another? Will he keep pace?

By early September, they were going back and forth. Sosa tied Big Mac at 48 homers in August, then McGwire surged ahead. On September 8, McGwire

TOP: Hall of Famer Andre "Hawk" Dawson came to Chicago after a standout turn in Montreal. He was the 1987 MVP with the Cubs and a five-time All-Star.

ABOVE: Say 'tweren't so, Sammy: Though Sosa thrilled Cubs fans with his homers and sprints to the outfield, accusations of using steroids derailed his legacy.

ended up being the first to reach the magic total of 62—in St. Louis against the Cubs, of course. Sosa himself would top the mark on September 13 at Wrigley Field. In fact, the two were tied with 66 homers on September 26. By the end of the season, however, McGwire added four more while Sosa added none. Once again, the Cubs finished second.

Sosa kept clubbing the ball, however, and hit 63 in 1999 and 64 in 2001. He became the first player ever with three 60-homer seasons, asterisk or no asterisk. He led the N.L. again in 2002 and left baseball in a cloud in 2005. But his exploits simply added to the allure of Wrigley Field as the place where homers fly.

It's worth mentioning here, too, that during this period Wrigley was the site of one of the greatest pitching performances in baseball history. On May 6, 1998, in a game against the Houston Astros at Wrigley, a fireballing righty rookie named Kerry Wood ("K" for Kerry) struck out 20 batters while walking only one and allowing only one hit. It was perhaps the most dominant game ever pitched.

The stunning early promise of Kerry Wood's career was derailed by injuries.

EVERYBODY LOVES WRIGLEY

Sosa's exploits, an increase in baseball's nostalgic appeal, and the sort of "lovable losers" that the Cubbies had become meant that Wrigley continued to rise in popularity. New ballparks popped up all over, but millions continued to look to Wrigley and Fenway as still better than the new, even when the Cubs squeezed in "luxury boxes" between the decks (and we use the term loosely; in the Cubbies' case, a luxury box is more akin to a balcony with walls, though the dessert cart is terrific). As more and more folks watched games there, the joy of the place spread.

The traditions that had been part of every Cubs fan's life for decades now went viral, even before YouTube.

It became a badge of baseball honor to take part in the scrums on Waveland Avenue battling for home-run balls behind the outfield walls. Even if a seat was available inside, thousands preferred to buy seats atop the buildings behind those walls, where wildcat bleachers arose as neighbors cashed in on the Cubbies' growing popularity. (The team tolerated the rooftop get-togethers, but when landlords began putting up bench seating and selling tickets, they stepped in; today a sort of truce exists of mutual support—that is, the Cubs get some of the money.) The bleacher creatures' serenading of hometown players spread to other ballparks, such as

ABOVE: When you sit beneath the big scoreboard in center, the Chicago skyline looms off to your left; to the right, you see the flatness of the prairie landscape. In front, you just see green.

ENCLOSED 1: Cute cubbies playing ball decorate this ticket from the 1932 World Series. The Yankees won this game 3, 7–5, on their way to sweeping Chicago.

ENCLOSED 2: Back in the Bronx, Yankees fans took home this World Series program; note the preprinted lineup on the scorecards.

Only in

WRIGLEY FIELD

- The ivy.

- Celebrities singing "Take Me Out to the Ballgame."

- The divisional flags in center field.

- The sign on the building outside right field reads "Eamus Catuli" ("Go Cubs!" in Latin).

- The giant red sign at the main entrance, installed in 1934, was blue until the 1960s.

- The fact that the team has never won a World Series while playing there.

- The crowds waiting on Waveland Avenue for batting-practice homers.

Yankee Stadium's famous first-inning greetings of New York players. And the rejection of opposing homers is now almost standard (unless the guy is, like, a really big star). By the late 1990s, lots of fans knew that the W and L flags that fly above the park signify a win or loss. They knew that the 14 and 26 flags that adorn the flagpoles were for Ernie Banks and Billy Williams. (Ron Santo, 10, Ryne Sandberg, 23, and Fergie Jenkins, 31, have since joined the original pair as their numbers were retired.) They know that a ball that gets stuck in the ivy is a ground-rule double (the only such rule in the big leagues).

But as happy as those times were—and Wrigley continues to bask, a decade-plus later, from that period of joy—there was one more dark cloud to hover over the ballpark, one accursed moment to join a retinue of others.

In 2003, the Cubs were as close as they had been in decades to finally returning to the World Series. At Wrigley Field, they led the Florida Marlins 3–0 in the eighth inning of game 6 of the N.L. Championship Series. They led the series three games to two, so they were thus five outs away from making the Fall Classic. The Marlins' Luis Castillo lofted a pop fly down the left field line; left fielder Moises Alou raced toward

the wall to make the grab. Jumping from the foul line, he reached up to snag the descending ball . . . and fans intervened. Hands reached out for the potential souvenir and knocked it away from Alou. He turned indignantly toward the fans, pointing and accusing. One fan in particular was later rather harshly called out as the villain of the piece, and the name Steve Bartman went down in baseball history. Castillo then, of course, reached base and the Cubs imploded, giving up eight runs in the inning and losing the game. They of course also lost game 7, and most of the Cubbie faithful blamed it on the billy goat, Bartman, and generally being the Cubs.

A couple of other recent sports events that took place at Wrigley are worth mentioning, both for their singularity and their classic Cubs-ness.

On January 1, 2009, the National Hockey League staged its Winter Classic outdoors on a rink built on the

TOP: It's a long way from these bleachers atop Waveland Avenue buildings to home plate, but the sight lines are clear and you can't beat the unique setting.

ABOVE: What might have been: Unlucky Steve Bartman (blue cap, reaching out) enters history by knocking a potential out away from the Cubs' Moises Alou in a 2003 playoff game.

Here's something most Cubs' fans' grandparents never saw: A night game at Wrigley. Not until 1988 did Wrigleyville, Chicago, and the Cubs bow to league pressure and install lights for night games.

Wrigley diamond. More than 40,000 fans braved the 30-degree temperatures, only to watch the hometown Chicago Blackhawks lose to the visiting Detroit Red Wings. Then, on November 20, 2010, Wrigley welcomed the Illinois-Northwestern college football game. Although numerous plans for this special game were made ahead of time, at the last minute it was decided that there was not enough space outside the field for player safety. The decision was made to use just one end zone; when the ball changed hands, the teams changed directions so that the offense was always going away from the brick outfield walls. The game turned into a PR disaster and many fans regarded it as a joke. It looked like that billy goat didn't like college football either.

Though football probably won't be back to Wrigley, baseball surely will be, season after season, as it has for coming up on a century. The fans will come to the neighborhood; the bleachers, inside and out, will fill with faithful; and the ghost of Harry Caray will boom out a greeting. Grandparents will show their grandkids where they sat when Banks hit a homer or where the Cubs almost won. They'll all watch together, confined in friendliness.

WRIGLEY FIELD
HOME OF
CHICAGO CUBS
WELCOME TO
OPENING NIGHT

★ ★

Purists still scoff, but night games at Wrigley have not upset the fabric of the universe, and in fact make it easier for many working folks to attend games at the venerable ballpark.

★

In a city filled with monumental buildings and splendid parks, Yankee Stadium combined both of those attributes like no other place on the island. Its massive structure dominated the nearby skyline, while its green grass sparkled for generations.

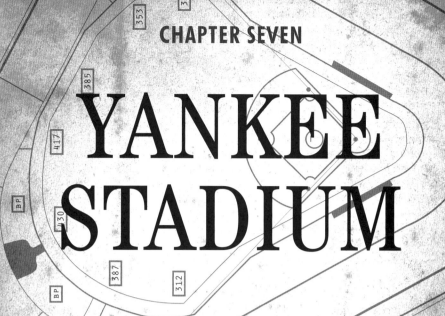

CHAPTER SEVEN

YANKEE STADIUM

BRONX, N.Y.

YEAR BUILT	1923
HOME TEAM	New York Yankees
FIRST GAME	April 18, 1923
LAST GAME	September 21, 2008
CAPACITY (AVERAGE)	56,000
FAMOUS FEATURES	Monument Park, scalloped architectural detail, massive size, decades of champions

It was just so big. It was enormous. It was colossal. And though they didn't know it when it was built, it had to be, to contain the decades of dominance and parade of heroes that would march through the Bronx over the next nine decades. It was the first baseball place to be called "Stadium." On its first day, it was the biggest in the sport. In the biggest city in the land, it was the biggest of its kind.

Cue Bob Sheppard, who was the P.A. voice there for more than 50 years:

"Welcome to . . . Yankee Stadium."

Compare this overhead shot to the previous page to see some of the changes that the stadium went through over the years. The most striking to note is the removal of the wide copper roof that overhung most of the stands.

The other subjects of our book had or have charm and moxie and ivy and bricks. Yankee Stadium dwarfed them all.

The other subjects hoped for an occasional glimpse of the World Series. Yankee Stadium played host to 33 Fall Classics.

The other ballparks were excited by a crowd of 40,000. Yankee Stadium, for a time at least, could top 80,000 if fans squeezed.

Everything about Yankee Stadium, from the players to the views to the fans' opinion of their team, was bigger.

Yankee Stadium started with beer and the Babe, it witnessed some of baseball's biggest moments, to say nothing of some pretty momentous football and boxing events, and it was throughout its life the perfect mix of team and building. Had the Cubs, for instance, played in Yankee Stadium, the ballpark wouldn't have made it through the 1950s.

A COLOSSUS RISES

The history of the Yankees—and one might say, the history of baseball—is divided into two periods: B.B.R. and A.B.R. Before Babe Ruth, the Yanks were an also-ran team, a second tenant in the Polo Grounds with the Giants, an afterthought still struggling to earn any traction. After Babe Ruth, the Giants were second-string in their own ballpark, soon took the Yankees' place as No. 2, and then even left the city.

Ruth joined the Yankees from the Red Sox for the 1920 season. Though primarily a lefty pitcher with Boston, he had 29 homers in 1919, his final season in Boston. In New York, he showed that he was just getting started. Helped by the short porch in right at the Polo Grounds, Ruth hit 29 home-field homers that season on his way to 54, a new league record. His Polo Grounds dingers were more than any other player hit, home *and* away. That was the good news. The bad news, for the landlords, that is, was that the Yankees far outdrew the Giants. In 1920, in Ruth's first season in New York, the Yankees became the first big-league club to top one million in attendance. John McGraw and John Brush had had enough and they began the process to kick the Yankees out. McGraw famously reckoned that since there was no more open land available in Manhattan, the Yanks would have to go to (gasp!) the Bronx, leaving the island free for Giant domination.

Not so fast, Mr. McGraw. Seeing the huge numbers of fans eager for a glimpse of Ruth and his pals, Yankees owners Jacob Ruppert and Tillinghast L'Hommedieu Huston (and if that impressive moniker was not enough,

LEFT: The metal skeleton of Yankee Stadium rises in 1922; the entire structure was built in less than a year by the White Construction Company.

ABOVE: Once this slugger got a hold of the place, however, White Co. was forgotten and Yankee Stadium became the House That Ruth Built.

both gents styled themselves as "Colonel," thanks to honorary ranks) knew they could build something a bit more than a quaint little park. A site in Long Island City was considered but fell through. A plan to build over the railroad tracks on the site of what became Madison Square Garden was rejected by the Army, which had designs on the area for antiaircraft guns. Finally, just across the East River from the Polo Grounds, they found a large tract that was part of fur fortune heir and politician William Astor's vast estates and picked it up

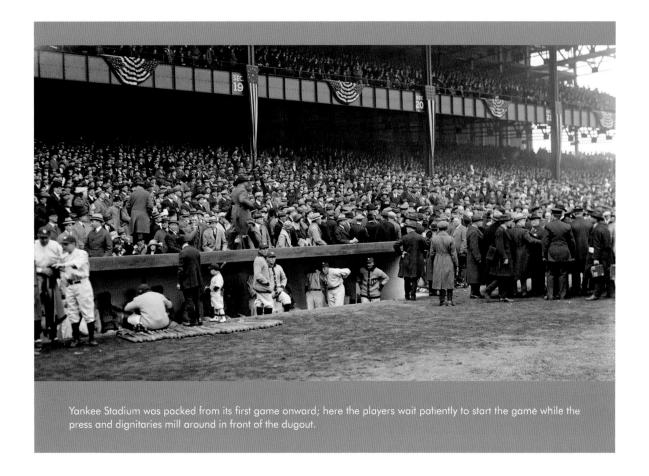

Yankee Stadium was packed from its first game onward; here the players wait patiently to start the game while the press and dignitaries mill around in front of the dugout.

for $675,000. The subway had recently been extended to reach the area, meaning fans could hop an uptown train with no problem.

Ruppert, who had made his fortune selling beer, and Huston, his right-hand man and an engineer himself, went way beyond the jewel boxes built before the war. Working with Osborn Engineering and White Construction Company, they graded 45,000 cubic yards of earth . . . they rolled in 3 million board-feet of lumber to make concrete forms . . . they used 950,000 board-feet of fir to make the bleachers . . . and they built all the other seats on site, using more than one million brass screws. (They were also nice enough to include eight bathrooms each for men and women.) And what did all that make? In the Roaring '20s, with New York booming and money flowing, they didn't dally with single decks and small bleachers and short capacities. In less than a year (284 days, to be exact), they constructed a behemoth of a ballpark, a soaring, mighty edifice that

rose three decks high above the playing field. About 55,000 fans could sit inside in comfort in those decks and in the bleachers across the outfield. Around the top edges of the stadium, they had a famous design frieze installed, made of copper that glinted in the sunlight and whose shape remains a part of the new Yankee Stadium that opened in 2010.

Opening day for Yankee Stadium could not have gone better had it been scripted and staged. Packing every corner of standing room and more, about 74,000 people crowded inside and reports said another 25,000 were turned away. Cars rolled into the nearby lots while subway trains disgorged the masses. Famed conductor John Philip Sousa himself led a marching band, while New York governor Al Smith threw out the first ball.

And with the baseball gods smiling down, Babe Ruth hit a three-run homer. The Yankees beat the Red Sox, 4–1. He topped off the stadium's first season by hitting three homers in the World Series, which the

The massive crowd attending opening day, 1923, Yankee Stadium's debut. **INSET:** Ruth greeted President Warren G. Harding that day.

Top 10 Moments at
YANKEE STADIUM

(in chronological order)

September 30, 1927
Babe Ruth hits his 60th homer of the season.

July 4, 1939
Lou Gehrig Day honors the Yankee slugger, who gives the most memorable speech in baseball.

July 2, 1941
Joe DiMaggio sets a new all-time record for consecutive games with a hit, with 45, on his way to a final mark of 56.

June 13, 1948
Babe Ruth says good-bye to baseball.

October 8, 1956
The Yankees' Don Larsen pitches the only perfect game in World Series history, a 2–0 game 5 victory over the Brooklyn Dodgers.

October 1, 1961
Roger Maris goes yard for the 61st time, breaking Ruth's record.

October 18, 1977
Three swings, three homers, and a new Yankees legend is born: Reggie Jackson, Mr. October, in game 6 of the World Series.

October 26, 1996
The Yankees win their first World Series in 18 years.

July 18, 1999
David Cone makes it three perfect games in stadium history, doing so in front of Don Larsen on Yogi Berra Day.

September 21, 2008
Yankee Stadium's last day is one of its most poignant, and also one of its most memorable.

This image from 1926 offers a great look at the vast sweep of the stadium and its triple decks. Note the classic scalloped detail along the top edge of the stands at the back.

Yankees won over the Giants. New York writer Fred Lieb wrote after opening day that the new stadium was "the House That Ruth Built."

You might also say it was the House Built *for* Ruth. Yankees owners, knowing that their left-handed slugger was a dead-pull hitter, made right field nearly as close as it was at the Polo Grounds, reportedly just over 250 feet away. However, the outfield swooped away to as deep as 500 feet at one point (though the walls moved in and out as seats were added over the years, moving to 408 by the time the stadium closed), curving back in toward the left field corner—an identical distance from home as in right.

CHAMPIONSHIPS AND FAREWELLS

After winning the World Series in their first season in Yankee Stadium, the ball club began a run of excellence unmatched in American sports. Over the next eight decades, they won an astounding 27 World Series, many of them ending with the home team dancing on the Yankee Stadium infield.

The first of those, after the inaugural season, came in 1927 with one of the most dominant teams of all time. They won 110 games and led the A.L. by 19 games, helped in large part by yet another Ruthian milestone. On September 30 of that season, Ruth hit a pitch from Washington's Tom Zachary into the

TOP: Ruth follows through as home run No. 60 of the 1927 season soars into the right field seats at Yankee Stadium. No one would top the mark for 34 years.
RIGHT: A few years earlier, Ruth had helped the Yankees hoist their first A.L. pennant after the 1923 season.

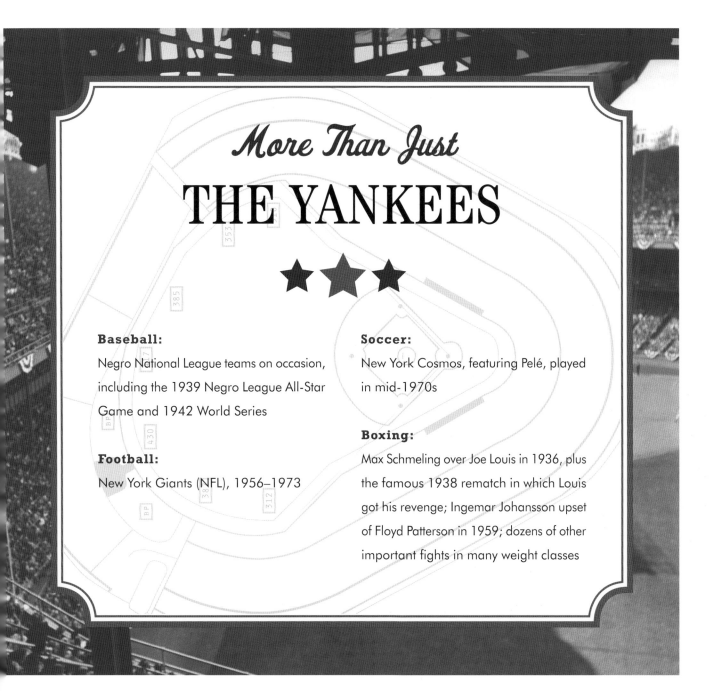

More Than Just
THE YANKEES
★ ★ ★

Baseball:

Negro National League teams on occasion, including the 1939 Negro League All-Star Game and 1942 World Series

Football:

New York Giants (NFL), 1956–1973

Soccer:

New York Cosmos, featuring Pelé, played in mid-1970s

Boxing:

Max Schmeling over Joe Louis in 1936, plus the famous 1938 rematch in which Louis got his revenge; Ingemar Johansson upset of Floyd Patterson in 1959; dozens of other important fights in many weight classes

right field seats, built conveniently close to home plate by Ruppert and Huston, knowing Ruth's pull-hitting power. That homer was No. 60 on the season, breaking his own record of 59 set in 1921 and establishing it as baseball's magic number.

Speaking of magic, another sports legend was made at the stadium in 1928, but not in baseball. College football games had been staged at the stadium since its first off-season in 1923. On November 10, 1928, Notre Dame played Army in a battle of two of the top teams in the country. At halftime, the Fighting Irish

trailed the Cadets, but coach Knute Rockne delivered a speech that entered the American lexicon. Referring to George Gipp, a former Notre Dame player who had died in 1920, Rockne told his team to "go out there and win one for the Gipper." Notre Dame did just that, beating Army 12–6 and adding a page to sports legend.

Back to baseball: The Yankees had won the World Series in 1927 in a sweep that concluded at Yankee Stadium. Ruth had two homers and seven RBI. His slugging partner Lou Gehrig, who himself had 47 homers that season, best by anyone ever not named

The first of the famous Yankee monuments was dedicated in 1932, in honor of the popular manager Miller Huggins, who had died from a blood infection in 1929.

Babe, hit .308. The twosome would lead the Yanks to another title in 1928 and a fourth in 1932. By 1936, the Yankees had added another legend, "Joltin' Joe" DiMaggio, the "Yankee Clipper." He joined Gehrig to lead the Yankees to four straight World Series titles (1936–1939).

Throughout this period, the stadium was evolving. One of the most lasting and important changes came in 1929 following the sudden death of manager Miller Huggins. The team put up a granite monument to the beloved skipper next to the flagpole that stood on the grass in play in center field. After Gehrig and later Ruth died, similar headstone-like monuments were erected. The trio remained a distinct feature of the diamond in the Bronx until 1976.

Also, the second and third decks had not extended past the foul pole in 1923, but by 1928 they had. In 1937, the wood bleachers had been swapped out for concrete, and capacity had risen to nearly 80,000. The stadium still didn't sport many frills or fancy amenities, but was often decorated with red-white-and-blue bunting to reflect the teams' all-American name as well as the

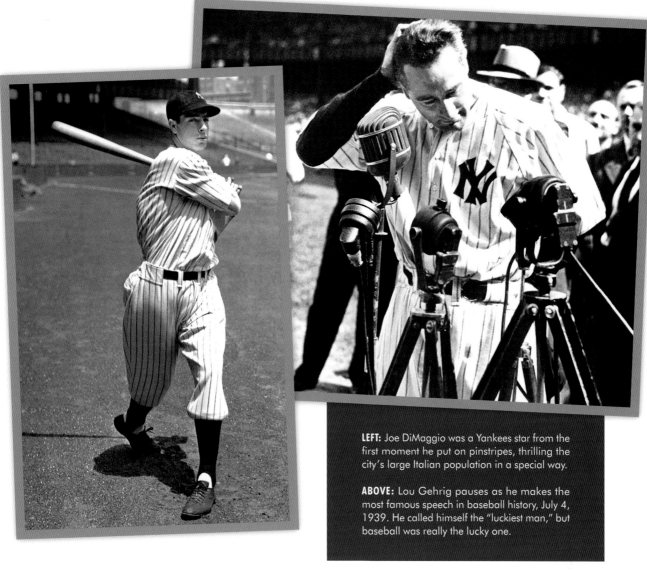

LEFT: Joe DiMaggio was a Yankees star from the first moment he put on pinstripes, thrilling the city's large Italian population in a special way.

ABOVE: Lou Gehrig pauses as he makes the most famous speech in baseball history, July 4, 1939. He called himself the "luckiest man," but baseball was really the lucky one.

frequent special events such as World Series games. Fans who came to Yankee Stadium weren't looking for any thrills except those on the field below them, but the visceral thrill of emerging from a long tunnel from the outer corridors into the green-carpeted expanse was one to remember.

Another non-baseball special event occurred in 1938, in the shadow of a looming European war. Two years earlier, heavyweight fighter Joe Louis had been beaten at the stadium by German boxer Max Schmeling. However, by '38, the rise of the Nazi regime in Germany was becoming world news and Schmeling, though he was not part of the Nazi party, was seen as its exemplar. Louis, though African American, had since become world champion and was seen as America's hope to

defeat the German. In an event charged with patriotic fervor, Louis knocked Schmeling down three times and the fight was over before the first round ended.

The stadium hosted its first All-Star Game in 1939, a summer that also saw one of the most famous events ever at Yankee Stadium, an event that would never appear in a box score. Gehrig, the much-loved Yankees star who had played 2,130 consecutive games until May of 1939, announced his retirement on Lou Gehrig Day, July 4, 1939. "The Iron Horse," stricken with ALS, the disease that would come to bear his name and would take his life two years later, gave a speech to a packed house that remains among sports' most admired. Though he knew he was sick with something and that his life's work in

TOP: The view from the very top of the right field seats, but any Yankees fan worth his pinstripes would have been thrilled to see this game 2 of the 1953 World Series.
ABOVE: In the locker room Hank Bauer, Yogi Berra, Billy Martin, and Joe Collins celebrate a win.

Only in
YANKEE STADIUM

★ ★ ★

- The first three-decker in the big leagues.

- Watching subway trains roll by on tracks beyond right field.

- In the renovated version, the broad expanse of scalloped design across the high outfield walls, recalling the former exterior detail.

- Monument Park: Some teams have tried to mimic it, but none can match the Yankees' amazing history.

baseball was ended, he nevertheless called himself "the luckiest man on the face of the earth." Surviving clips of his speech captured the silence that surrounded him as he spoke as well as the echo of his words in the vast stadium, words that continue to echo through the years.

LIGHTS SHINE ON A DOMINANT ERA

Yankee Stadium remained open for baseball during World War II, though many of its star players, including DiMaggio, left to join the service. In 1946, the stadium added lights for the first time, joining an ongoing big-league trend. Army and Notre Dame played another memorable game in 1946, too, ending in a 0–0 tie. And in 1948, Babe Ruth said good-bye to the stadium he "built." Frail and ill, steadying himself with a bat as a cane, he spoke words less-remembered than Gehrig's, but just as heartfelt, to a stadium filled with his admirers. Two months later, more than 100,000 of those admirers lined up to walk by his casket as it lay in state at Yankee Stadium.

After Ruth's death, the Yankees embarked on a dynasty unmatched in the 130-plus years of pro baseball. Beginning in 1949, they won five straight World Series. Three of those championships, 1950, 1951, and 1953, were captured at Yankee Stadium itself.

Slide, Mickey, slide! In his remarkable 18-year career in the Bronx, Mantle won three MVP Awards and was named an All-Star 16 times, while helping the Yanks win seven World Series.

DiMaggio was part of the first three, but he retired after 1951. But the next great transcendent star was already on board to take his place. Mickey Mantle, the "Commerce Comet," a slugging switch-hitter and so fleet of foot, joined the Yankees in DiMaggio's last year. His boyish charm, his blond good looks, and his otherworldly skills made him the toast of the town. Though a knee injury suffered when he tripped on a drain in the Yankee Stadium outfield during the 1951 World Series would slow him slightly and other injuries would sap his speed, Mantle's amazing career included

16 All-Star Games, three MVP Awards, 536 homers, and a series of tape-measure homers still talked about with awe. Like Ruth and DiMaggio, Mantle made Yankee Stadium his personal playground, attracting millions of fans to the Bronx.

He was the big bopper on an amazing unit that also included three-time MVP catcher Yogi Berra. Later a Yankees manager and baseball icon, Berra in the 1950s was a slow-footed, hard-hitting player who was a perfect complement to Mantle's speedy style. On the mound, Whitey Ford led the way. The "Chairman of the Board"

set a still-standing record with 10 wins in World Series play. Shortstop Phil Rizzuto, "the Scooter," won an MVP of his own and later became the team's longtime and oft-quoted ("Holy cow!") broadcaster. At the helm was the Old Perfessor, Casey Stengel, the former Brooklyn Dodgers player. Stengel juggled his cast of all-stars to the greatest run of success in baseball history. In fact, the team not only won five straight World Series, they played in seven out of ten, also winning in 1956.

In the 1956 World Series, the stadium was witness to another singular event. In game 2 of the series, journeyman pitcher Don Larsen had gotten shelled, leaving in the second inning. In game 5, however, Stengel sent him back out for another try at the cross-town rival Brooklyn Dodgers. Larsen famously reported that he did not learn of this starting assignment until he arrived at the ballpark and found a baseball in his shoe, Stengel's signal to get to work. Larsen proceeded

to shut down a Dodgers lineup that included four Hall of Famers in a manner unlike any World Series pitcher before or since. Larsen threw the only perfect game in postseason history, winning 2–0, helped by a Mantle home run. The image of Berra leaping into Larsen's arms after the final out—a called strike three to pinch hitter Dale Mitchell in his last career at-bat, trivia fans—is one of Yankee Stadium's most indelible. Though recent seasons have seen a strange burst of perfection (five perfectos were pitched from 2009 to 2012), Larsen's

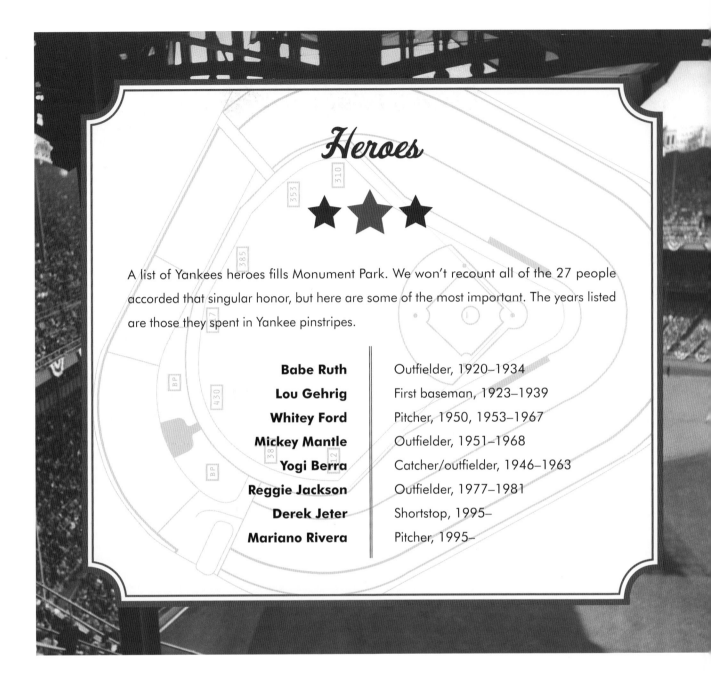

Heroes

★ ★ ★

A list of Yankees heroes fills Monument Park. We won't recount all of the 27 people accorded that singular honor, but here are some of the most important. The years listed are those they spent in Yankee pinstripes.

Babe Ruth	Outfielder, 1920–1934
Lou Gehrig	First baseman, 1923–1939
Whitey Ford	Pitcher, 1950, 1953–1967
Mickey Mantle	Outfielder, 1951–1968
Yogi Berra	Catcher/outfielder, 1946–1963
Reggie Jackson	Outfielder, 1977–1981
Derek Jeter	Shortstop, 1995–
Mariano Rivera	Pitcher, 1995–

remains the pinnacle of pitching success for timing, location, and historic import.

Another iconic moment occurred in the stadium two years later, but this time it was football that played its own sort of perfect game. The New York Giants had taken up residence in Yankee Stadium starting in 1956, winning the NFL title in their first season there. In 1958, they played host to the Baltimore Colts in the NFL Championship Game, the first to be nationally televised. As it turned out, that audience saw what is still called "the Greatest Game Ever Played." A thrilling, back-and-forth affair that saw several lead changes, the game was tied at the end of regulation after a last-second Colts field goal. Baltimore quarterback Johnny Unitas had led his team on one of his patented "two-minute drill" drives to tie the game. Now Yankee Stadium fans and those watching at home got to see the first overtime game in NFL history. In the end, Baltimore's Alan Ameche bulled in from the one-yard line to end the game. The game was thrilling by itself, but the impact it had on sports fans was bigger. The long and fruitful marriage between football and TV started that day in Yankee Stadium—think of that next time you enjoy a Sunday's worth of NFL games.

OFFICIAL PROGRAM - FIFTY CENTS

Yankees

YANKEE STADIUM

WORLD 1956 SERIES

BL-238-56

Dodgers

BBETS FIELD

★ ★

TOP: This swing gave Roger Maris 61 homers in 1961, topping Ruth's 60 in 1927 to the dismay of some and the delight of others. **ABOVE:** Maris was not even in the Majors when the Yankees won the 1956 World Series; the program shows managers Casey Stengel and Walter Alston.

★

to knock Ruth out of the top spot, Mantle and teammate Roger Maris staged a season-long home-run duel. The "M&M" boys thrilled fans wherever they went, but nowhere more so than at the stadium. As the duo raced toward Ruth's mark, some oldsters muttered that the record could not be broken due to the longer season and the fact that there were more—and thus diluted—teams. Regardless, on the final day of the season, Mantle having fallen out injured with 54 dingers, Maris clubbed a ball from Boston's Tracy Stallard into the right field seats for his 61st homer. The record stood until Mark McGwire and Sammy Sosa topped it in 1998. Maris was named the MVP and the Yankees cruised to yet another World Series title.

RENOVATION AND RETURN TO GLORY

In 1966, the stadium got a bit of a face-lift, with an all-white paint scheme added on the outside, and all the interior seats being painted blue. But it was just a quick brush-up, perhaps in anticipation of what was to come in the next decade.

The legendary moments just kept coming. Three years after that greatest game, Yankee Stadium was the home to the greatest home run season yet. Daring

Meanwhile, Mantle got his own monument out in center field, this one a plaque that joined DiMaggio's on the outfield wall. It was presented on Mickey Mantle Day in 1969. Playing the organ on Mickey Mantle Day, it is worth mentioning, is a man who would be a part of the place until he retired in 2003. To some regular visitors to the stadium, Eddie Layton was as much a part of the stadium as the grass. At his organ high above the playing field, he gave expression to the fans' joys and sorrows, inspired cheering, or simply entertained between innings in an era before teams insisted that loud music was the key to fans' pleasure at the yard. That day, P.A. man Sheppard was already 18 years into his 50-year career. Until he finally retired in 2007, his booming voice was as much a part of any fans' experience of the stadium as watching the subway cars roll past behind the right field wall.

The stadium by this point was still grand, it was an icon, yes, but it was utilitarian. It didn't have the charm of Fenway or Wrigley or the neighborhood-bar outlook of Ebbets. It was too big to be cuddly, too plain, for the most part, to be uniquely beautiful. It was the big kid on the block, comfortable and happy with just being bigger than anyone else. But it was getting old, it was cracking and leaking and was not up to the standards of the newer parks being built around the league by cities hoping to make their local teams happy.

In 1973, the team got a new owner who soon demanded that his new city do the same. Cleveland shipping magnate George Steinbrenner (who rather disingenuously said upon taking ownership that he would be an absentee owner and stick to building ships . . . ha!) basically threatened to take the Yankees out of New York if the city didn't pony up money to renovate the old stadium. In the end, the city agreed and it paid $160 million to upgrade the place in 1974–1975. The

Day One

Yankee Stadium Opens

"Up on the banks of the Harlem River yesterday afternoon, 'Babe' Ruth opened a new baseball park known as the Yankee Stadium. With something like 65,000 fans—the greatest crowd that ever saw a big league game of ball—looking on, 'Babe' in the third inning dedicated the new Yankee home with a four-base drive into the right field bleachers with two mates on."

New York Daily News, April 19, 1923

third deck was rebuilt entirely. Wooden seats that had seen Ruth and Gehrig play were replaced with blue plastic ones. The copper frieze was removed, but the scalloped shape was retained and copied in a band across the top of the outer wall behind the bleachers. Steel supports

While subway cars rumbling along the tracks (across lower part of image) could once be seen from the stands, the 1976 renovation closed up that view.

for the upper deck were removed, clearing obstructed views. A large scoreboard in the outfield had one of the big leagues' first video screens. Though capacity went down a bit to 54,000, the overall improvements gave the old place a new life. During the construction, the Yankees played their home games across the river in Queens at the Mets' Shea Stadium.

With construction completed, Yankee Stadium 1.5 opened for business again on April 15, 1976. As the 1923 team did, they opened with a win, this time 11–4 over Minnesota. Then, as the '23 team had, the Bronx Bombers christened the new field by arranging to play host to a World Series in October. To get there, however, they had to fight their own fans. After the Yanks

won the A.L. pennant on a dramatic homer by Chris Chambliss, all hell broke loose. Yankees fans starved for a title—the team hadn't been in the World Series since 1964—stormed the field. Chambliss had to make like one of the football Giants during a broken-field run that remains a baseball classic. New York lost the series to Cincinnati's "Big Red Machine," but big Octobers were still ahead for the team.

That first year of the renovated stadium saw another famous boxing match, one of 30 championship bouts held over the years. Though some joked that only Yankee Stadium was big enough to hold his personality, Muhammad Ali backed it up by beating Ken Norton to defend his heavyweight title. A famous publicity

photo shows the boxers chasing each other in the outfield during the days leading up to the fight.

Another gigantic personality found his moment in the Yankee Stadium spotlight the following fall. Reggie Jackson had joined the Yankees from the A's in 1976 and he immediately put his stamp on the ball club, saying he was "the straw that stirs the drink" in the wild-and-wacky team atmosphere famously labeled the "Bronx Zoo." But, as the saying goes, it ain't bragging if you back it up. On October 18, 1977, Jackson made baseball history and earned his "Mr. October" nickname. After walking in the first inning, Jackson saw three more pitches in game 6 of the World Series. He hit all three for home runs into the right field bleachers at the stadium. It was an epic performance, the first triple-homer series game since, you guessed it, Babe Ruth himself. That Jackson did what he did in the mighty confines of Yankee Stadium

LEFT: Chris Chambliss slugged a homer in game 5 of the 1976 ALCS to send the Yanks back to their accustomed place in the World Series.

ABOVE: The following year, Reggie Jackson made history with his three-homer game 6 performance, helping the Yankees win the first of two straight World Series.

seemed only fitting; only its vast size could contain both his talent and his ego.

The Yankees won again in 1978, but the joy of that win disappeared during the next season due to the death in a plane crash of beloved catcher Thurman Munson. The grumpy-looking field leader of the team, Munson had his number retired and joined the growing number

A Rookie of the Year and later an MVP, catcher Thurman Munson was the Yankees' captain for three World Series teams, including two champions. His death in 1979 shocked all of baseball.

of honorees in Monument Park behind left field. During the stadium's renovation, the on-field monuments and outfield wall plaques had been removed from the field and installed in a special area behind the wall. Fans could now visit the monuments, see plaques and signs honoring retired numbers, and just generally bask in the Yankee-ness of it all. Side note: Fans wearing Red Sox gear were strongly advised not to visit Monument Park (or perhaps even show up in the Bronx on any game day).

THE FINAL CURTAIN

Though the 1980s were a rare quiet decade in Yankee Stadium, the 1990s brought back all the glory . . . and then some. In 1993, pitcher Jim Abbott threw a no-hitter for the Yankees. A great feat, sure, but one of three no-nos that season and part of what has become the Yankees' all-time total of 11. So what made Abbott's special is that the lefty was born without a right hand. His amazing athleticism allowed him to forge a 10-year

ABOVE: Notice how Yankees lefty Jim Abbott is holding his glove as he throws a no-hitter in 1993: He'll have that glove on his left hand in a split second, since the remarkable pitcher was born without a right hand.

ENCLOSED 1: The holder of this ticket to game 6 of the 1953 World Series saw second baseman Billy Martin hit a walk-off RBI single in the bottom of the ninth to win the game and the series.

ENCLOSED 2: A hand-colored postcard offers a perhaps overly decorated view of the stadium from the right field seats.

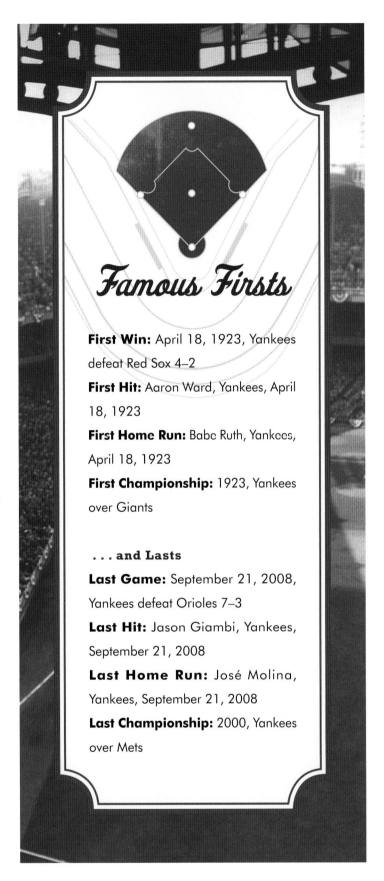

Famous Firsts

First Win: April 18, 1923, Yankees defeat Red Sox 4–2

First Hit: Aaron Ward, Yankees, April 18, 1923

First Home Run: Babe Ruth, Yankees, April 18, 1923

First Championship: 1923, Yankees over Giants

. . . and Lasts

Last Game: September 21, 2008, Yankees defeat Orioles 7–3

Last Hit: Jason Giambi, Yankees, September 21, 2008

Last Home Run: José Molina, Yankees, September 21, 2008

Last Championship: 2000, Yankees over Mets

Three years later, the unique layout of the Yankees' right field wall would turn the tide in a postseason game and help New York return to the World Series for the first time in 14 years. Here's the situation: Yankees trail the Orioles by a run, bottom of the eighth of the first game of the ALCS. Derek Jeter floats a fly ball to right field. Baltimore's Tony Tarasco camps under it right at the wall. Just then, because the seats at that spot are smack-dab next to the wall, a kid named Jeffrey Maier reached out and snagged the ball, pulling it into the stands. The umpires ruled that there was no fan interference, and Jeter circled the bases. Maier, meanwhile, achieved permanent hero status in the Big Apple. The Yanks went on to win the game in extras, they won the series over the Braves, and third baseman Wade Boggs rode around the outfield on the back of a police horse during the celebration. And in part because Maier got a front-row seat.

Remember Larsen? He was an alumnus of Point Loma High School in San Diego. On May 17, 1998, another Point Loman threw a perfect game at Yankee Stadium. David Wells, a player who so loved the Yankees that he once bought Babe Ruth's old hat at an auction and tried to wear it in a game, twirled his gem against the Twins. That season was also the start of another Yankees three-peat, which they capped off with a 2000 Subway Series win over the New York Mets.

The middle season of that streak saw an event that brought together all the Yankees ghosts and legends on one magical, numerically amazing afternoon. July 18, 1999, was Yogi Berra Day in the Bronx, honoring the longtime Yankee legend and ending a longstanding feud between Berra and Steinbrenner. Perfect-game pitcher Don Larson threw out the ceremonial first pitch, which Berra caught. Then David Cone threw out the rest. The Yankees' right hander used 88 pitches to craft

big-league career anyway, and his no-hitter was one of baseball's great feel-good stories. He threw it at the stadium against the Indians on September 4.

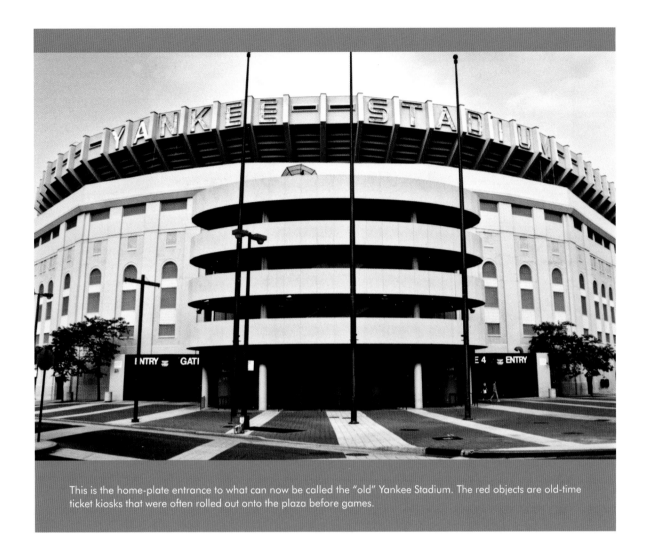

This is the home-plate entrance to what can now be called the "old" Yankee Stadium. The red objects are old-time ticket kiosks that were often rolled out onto the plaza before games.

a perfect game in the presence of the man who made them famous. Only at Yankee Stadium indeed. . . .

From Ruth and Gehrig to DiMaggio and Mantle to Jackson and Jeter . . . Yankee Stadium had seen the great ones. Joe Louis, the Greatest Game, even the Pope, had made history there. But perhaps the stadium's most emotional moment in all its decades came on September 25, 2001. Just two weeks earlier, terrorists had shocked the world with their brazen attacks on the United States. New York City was hardest hit, of course, as the Twin Towers fell. As it had done during World War II, the nation's eyes turned toward its national game for respite and relief. And what more fitting place to honor the fallen and begin the psychological rebuilding than at Yankee Stadium? As fans in tears filled the stadium, a massive American flag decorated the field, players wore

caps honoring local first responders, a silent prayer was said, and President George W. Bush threw out the first pitch. It was just a game, but it meant so much more.

That memorable event was somewhat of a last hurrah for Yankee Stadium. Yes, the team played in the World Series again in 2003, but they lost it. And marvelous players like Derek Jeter and Mariano Rivera and Andy Pettitte added their names to the long roster of Yankees immortals. But the stadium itself was not immortal. Even after its mid-1970s renovation, it had aged rapidly. It was still a great park, but it was a great *old* park. The place kind of smelled no matter where you went, and its closed-concourse plan gave it the feel of a warehouse until you got to your seat. Add to that the lack of space to add more of the luxury boxes and amenities that modern fans (and sponsors) were enjoying at other

The beginning of the end: This photo captures the massive crowd watching Andy Pettitte throw the first pitch of the last game at the House That Ruth Built, on September 21, 2008.

ballparks, and the writing was on the outfield wall. It was time for a new Yankee Stadium.

Plans were made, calendars set, a countdown clock ticked into gear in 2008, the last year of "old" Yankee Stadium. Fans packed the park all season for one more trip down memory lane, setting a new stadium attendance mark of more than 4.3 million. For one last time, they made their way inside, through the unadorned concrete tunnels and walkways, up a wide ramp, and to their sections. Entering the narrow passageway that led to the seats, they awaited again that magical feeling they had when their folks took them to their first game, that sudden flash of green amid the gray that signaled they'd arrived. And then they emerged,

the grass spreading out like a vast sea, the seats rising above in a massive curling wave, the sibilant murmur bursting into full-throated roar.

Yankee Stadium. Just saying it makes you shiver—especially if you were an opponent during their dominant years.

Yankee Stadium. One of a kind when it was built . . . one of a kind to the end.

The last night was as magical as one would expect at the place known as the Cathedral to some. Whereas the Polo Grounds and Ebbets Field went out with a whimper and Tiger Stadium with the clenched teeth of sad fans, Yankee Stadium strode proudly to its end, monumental, dignified, glorious. Before the game, on

September 21, 2008, a host of Yankee alumni or their family members jogged out to their positions one last time. Dignitaries saluted the place, baseball royalty gave their blessing.

The game itself was a series of lasts—homer, hit, pitch, out. And then, it was over—and yes, the Yankees won, beating Baltimore 7–3. After home plate was removed to be carried to the new stadium rising right next door, the lights were slowly put out. The 2008 team gathered on the infield to wave good-bye to their home and to their fans. In the dimness, a spotlight caught the captain, Derek Jeter, the embodiment of nine decades of pinstriped purpose. Though he said it was off-the-cuff, his speech at that moment was perfect. We can't do it any better.

For all of us up here, it's a huge honor to put this uniform on every day and come out here and play. And every member of this organization, past and present, has been calling this place home for 85 years. There's a lot of tradition, a lot of history, and a lot of memories. Now the great thing about memories is you're able to pass it along from generation to generation.

And although things are going to change next year, we're going to move across the street, there are a few things with the New York Yankees that never change—its pride, its tradition, and most of all, we have the greatest fans in the world. We're relying on you to take the memories from this stadium and add them to the new memories that come to the new Yankee Stadium, and continue to pass them on from generation to generation. On behalf of this entire organization, we want to take this moment to salute you, the greatest fans in the world.

IMAGE CREDITS

Unless otherwise stated below, all images courtesy of the National Baseball Hall of Fame Library, Cooperstown, N.Y.

Page 2: Carol M. Highsmith Archive, Library of Congress, Prints and Photographs Division

Page 8: Library of Congress Prints and Photographs Division

Page 10: Library of Congress Prints and Photographs Division

Page 12 (lower): Library of Congress Prints and Photographs Division

Page 26: Library of Congress Prints and Photographs Division

Page 57 (main): Marcio Silva/iStockphoto

Page 58 (left): Getty Images

Page 62 (main): Joyce Vincent/Shutterstock

Page 65: Rick Friedman/Corbis

Page 66 (upper): Jason Tench/Shutterstock

Page 76: Library of Congress Prints and Photographs Division

Page 83 (lower): Library of Congress Prints and Photographs Division

Page 101: George Grantham Bain Collection, Library of Congress

Page 122 (lower): John Livzey/Getty Images

Page 127 (lower): George Grantham Bain Collection, Library of Congress

Page 129: Library of Congress Prints and Photographs Division

Page 143 (upper): David Hodges/Alamy

Page 143 (lower): Getty Images

Page 145: Panoramic Images/Getty Images

Page 146: Carol M. Highsmith Archive, Library of Congress, Prints and Photographs Division

Page 150: George Grantham Bain Collection, Library of Congress

Page 151 (inset): George Grantham Bain Collection, Library of Congress

Page 172: Getty Images

Page 176: Gary Yim/Shutterstock

SOURCES

Among the many resources consulted by the author are the following. Their great scholarship and depth of detail greatly aided in the preparation of this manuscript. (Also, thanks to John Thorn for a last-minute save out of the research bull pen.)

Baseball: An Illustrated History, by Geoffrey C. Ward and Ken Burns (Knopf, 2000)

Baseball: The Golden Age, by Harold Seymour (Oxford University Press, 1971)

Ballparks Then and Now, by Eric Enders (Thunder Bay, 2002)

Diamonds: The Evolution of the Ballpark, by Michael Gershman (Houghton Mifflin, 1993)

Fenway Park, by John Powers and Ron Driscoll (Running Press, 2012)

Green Cathedrals, by Philip J. Lowry (SABR/Walker & Co., 2006)

Lost Ballparks, by Lawrence S. Ritter (Studio, 1994)

Red Sox Century, by Glenn Stout and Richard A. Johnson (Houghton Mifflin, 2000)

A Yankee Stadium Scrapbook, by David Fischer (Running Press, 2008)

MLB.com (and affiliated team sites)

ESPN.com

Baseball-reference.com

Retrosheet.com

SportingNews.com

ABOUT THE AUTHOR

JAMES BUCKLEY JR. is the author of many books on sports history, including *The Baseball Hall of Fame Collection*, *Treasures of the National Football League*, *Perfect: The Story of Baseball's 20 Perfect Games* (yes, it was published before 2012's spate of perfectos—watch for an update!), *Unhittable*, *Eyewitness Baseball*, and *Sports Immortals*. After working at *Sports Illustrated* and NFL Publishing, he founded a book producer and editorial services company, the Shoreline Publishing Group, in 2000. Shoreline has since created more than 300 books and magazines on sports and many other topics. He is on the board of directors of a four-time national-champion college summer-ball team, the Santa Barbara (California) Foresters.

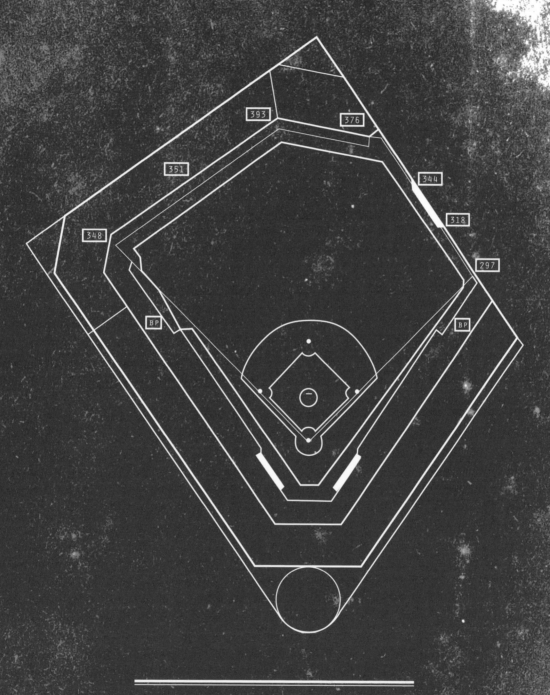

EBBETS FIELD

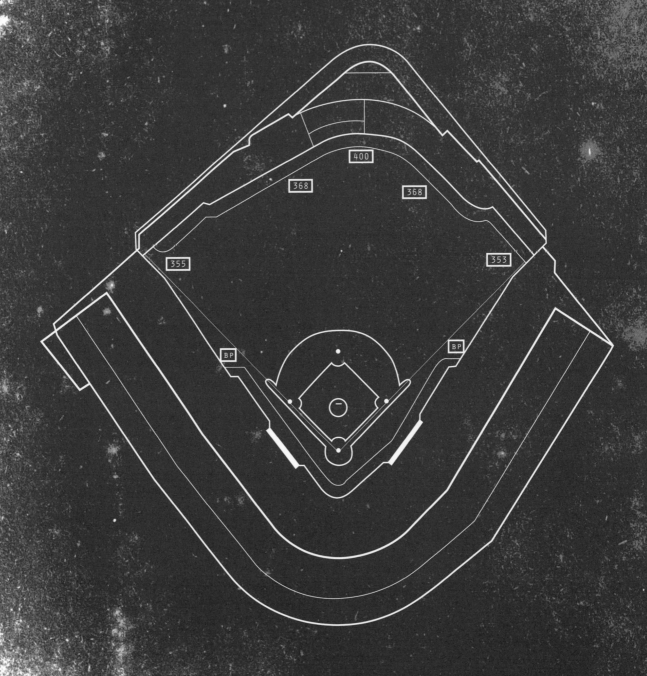

WRIGLEY FIELD